Pretty Dark Places

Transforming Trauma, Healing Addiction, and Cultivating an Empowered Life

CHRYSTAL LEE

Pretty Dark Places

Transforming Trauma, Healing Addiction, and Cultivating an Empowered Life

CHRYSTAL LEE

Pretty Dark Publishing

Pretty Dark Places
First edition: January 15, 2025
Production, cover design, and layout by Liquet.co
© 2025, Chrystal Lee
www.prettydarkplaces.com
ISBN 978-1-0691639-0-5

Acknowledgments

There are a great number of people to whom I am grateful for their help on my journey. This book wouldn't be possible were it not for some beautiful souls I have been incredibly fortunate to have in my life. To begin, I want to acknowledge and dedicate this work to my four beautiful children. Each of you is extraordinary and a gift from Yahusha above. I love you all dearly.

I want to dedicate this book to my wonderful sister, Lisa, who was tasked, far too often, with being a surrogate mother to me in our youth. It is not fair, the responsibilities that were placed on your shoulders; still, I am forever grateful to you for continually being a source of guidance and nurturing to me. Lisa, I love you and would not be here today if it were not for you; thank you.

To my best friends of thirty years, Karla and Angelina, thank you for never judging me and always being there as an incredible support system. I love you forever.

Finally, I dedicate this in loving memory of three important men: first, my dearly departed brother, Jonathan (May 13, 1975 – May 19, 2022). You have been my greatest teacher. Your own battles with addiction helped to change my own understanding. Secondly, my nephew and Jonathan's son, Colton Allen (October 19, 1996 - November 16, 2024). Colton, I'm so sorry that I couldn't get to you in time. And thirdly for Alain, my best friend, and greatest love. Our time together here on earth was cut far too short. There is not a day that goes by where I don't hear your voice telling me: "Chrystal, do the next right thing." Until we meet again, you are always in my heart.

Table of Contents

Foreward

When I first considered writing this book, I wanted to make sure I told my story in a way that accurately reflected my unique experiences and provided practical help to readers. Each of us has a story, and we all experience hardship in life. When I started to reflect on my own hardships, I realized the best way of making meaning out of the things I've experienced is to share my insights with others.

My unique experiences and perspective, however, should provide both comfort and practical insights for those experiencing hardship, especially single moms, those affected by trauma, and those interested in how plant-based medicine can promote recovery.

This book is part memoir and part narrative guide. I don't just want to tell my story; I want to do so in a way that helps you better understand how to navigate your own challenges and individual recovery from addiction, shame, and trauma. All of us have been, and continue to be, affected by various traumas - from the trauma we all experience as children, to the trauma that life throws at us as adults. Trauma is, unfortunately, part of life. Trauma does not have to define you, however. As I've learned throughout my journey, life is not so much about what happens to you; it's about how you respond to the things you're affected by. How do you frame your experiences? Do you see yourself in passive terms, powerless against the challenges that affect you? Or do you see yourself as powerful, having agency and a strong will to fight – especially when a fight lands on your doorstep through no fault of your own?

Single moms are used to challenges; we thrive on the satisfaction and fulfillment of rising to the occasion and caring for those closest to us. I want to make clear, however, that this book isn't just for single mothers or those who can personally relate to the specific challenges and situations I describe here. Suppose you're interested in plant medicine but come from a different perspective than mine. In that case, you can still take so much away from my experiences concerning healing addiction and dealing with trauma. Suppose you're battling addiction but come from a very different perspective regarding what perpetuates your behavior. The information and lessons I present here are relevant for anyone battling any kind of addiction.

From the outset of this book, I want to make clear that while I outline several serious life challenges that have been externally imposed, I am neither a victim nor a martyr. This book isn't about airing grievances or expressing hostility – even to those I believe have acted maliciously toward me. Holding hatred or resentment in your heart only degrades your own health and happiness. I try to look back with understanding, even in cases where it probably would be fair to hold a little resentment. Resentment does nothing for me and doesn't negatively impact those who wronged me. At the same time, I want to clarify that I won't pull any punches or sugarcoat the truth. This story is raw and real. Parts of it are sad, parts of it are hilarious, but all of it is critically important to understand my journey and why I'm even here today. In sharing this raw truth with you, the reader, I want us both to develop genuine understanding. Such understanding can only come from the raw and honest truth.

Whether you know me or not, I want this book to provide a genuine window into my life. This is important not just so strangers can understand and benefit from my experiences but also for my children, parents, and those closest to me. Allowing yourself to be defined by others' narratives of yourself – especially when these ideas don't reflect the truth, or at least the complete truth, is harmful. It harms not only your physical and spiritual self but also your loved ones, who may internalize the wrong ideas about who you are or why you responded in a particular way to a given situation. At the same time, holding myself accountable for the mistakes that I have made is critically important to my own spiritual and emotional growth. It is also a critically important lesson for my children, who are my heart.

So, I'm writing this book for others, first and foremost, but I'm also writing for myself. I've heard it said that writing a memoir is one of the most effective forms of therapy there is. Telling my story in a way that truly captures these experiences and what it means to have experienced these things is important. For all of these reasons, I don't pull punches or filter the truth. Addiction, trauma, shame, and recovery are powerful topics and issues. Even for those not impacted by these issues in our own lives, many of our loved ones are. I don't promise answers or total understanding, but I do promise to present an honest and accurate accounting of events and the insights I've gained in recovery. The applicability of these insights certainly will depend on who you are and where you're at in your own journey, but as I've noted, I've strived to make the information in this book as universal as possible.

The major catalyst for my writing this book was the sudden loss of my brother. He died on May 19th, 2022. He had lifelong struggles with addiction and related issues, but his death was a shock, and it had a profound impact on me. Ask anyone who's ever been in the unfortunate position: the sudden loss of a loved one tends to remind you of your limited time on this earth and your need to pursue your best possible life. Being honest with yourself and being honest with those around you is critical for leading such a life.

I've also come to learn that sharing our experiences with others can help give greater meaning to our and their lives. Anyone who's experienced any kind of trauma will also know that talking about our experiences helps promote healing – both our own and others. Through sharing these experiences, I hope to be more connected to not just my immediate family and the people in my life but also others who I don't know but for whom my experiences might be helpful in navigating their own challenges and difficulties.

As a note of caution, my particular journey toward healing from trauma and addiction has involved plant medicine. I want to clarify, however, that just because plant medicine helped me, does not make it right for you, necessarily. Plant medicine is serious and should be taken seriously. I've tried to present my experiences with all the wonder and humor appropriate, and I want readers to be entertained. But I do not want to trivialize these experiences or the profound impact that these ceremonies can have, especially for those of us struggling with addiction. So, while I am grateful for my experiences with plant medicine and would recommend it to many people dealing with various challenges and ailments, I would also caution anyone interested to do as much research as possible using legitimate, authoritative sources. Plant medicine is neither a quick fix nor a plaything to be trifled with.

Most of this book is ordered chronologically based on the order in which particular events happen, with the exception of the opening chapter. On January 9th, 2018, I was falsely arrested for a crime I didn't commit, which ultimately led to addictions involving alcohol and cocaine. While my false arrest was a major catalyst for addiction in my life, it certainly isn't the start of my story, nor a means to explain entirely the trauma that underpinned my addictions. So, while I start with the arrest and all the chaos and anxiety that accompanied it, from there, I go back and take you through my childhood and relationships with family to adulthood, marriage, divorce, and ultimately the sequence of events that would lead to my false arrest and my eventual vindication with all charges dropped.

As you'll learn, however, this bizarre and, at times, fantastic sequence of events would make up just one facet of a larger and, I believe, much more universal and important story – a story about trauma, shame, addiction, and recovery.

So why are we here? I have a story to tell. My sharing of my story of recovery from addiction is to help empower you and show you the beautiful possibilities that arise when we allow ourselves the space to heal from our shame and trauma, which ultimately drive and fuel our addictive behaviors. You don't come through what I've been through without some real knowledge and insight. I am sharing these lessons with the world because I desperately want to help anyone facing similar challenges in life. And, as I've learned – many of these challenges are universal. Still, I speak purely from my own experience and perspective and remind readers to take what applies and disregard what does not, based on their own unique situation. With such an approach, we can successfully navigate these Pretty Dark Places together.

One: Getting Arrested Changes Your Life

I don't know if you've ever done any public speaking, but it can be a thrilling, gratifying experience. Getting up and speaking in front of a large group of people tends to cause a little stress for most of us, even for the most experienced public speakers. That normal, healthy stress is just about us wanting to do a good job, to connect with our audiences, and to feel understood. Personally, however, I've never felt much stress — I love public speaking. I shine when I can connect with an individual or a group over something I'm passionate about. For me, it's exhilarating to prepare to speak; I think about the words I'll use, and ensure my outfit, hair, and makeup are just right. I reflect on how I'll share my passion with others and, hopefully, help them in some way. It isn't just exciting, it's enthralling. I love connecting with others; it makes me feel alive. The day I have a public speaking engagement, I'm excited and filled with a sense of delight.

On January 9, 2018, I was in just such a mindset. I was scheduled to speak at a local hotel lounge that evening. Giving talks like these was such a positive experience for me. I felt like I was sharing useful, valuable information with those just like myself – those who could benefit from my unique knowledge in a new and exciting opportunity. And it wasn't my first rodeo, either. In recent months, I'd found myself in the position of proselytizer for something that had emerged as a real blessing in my life — gifting circles. For the uninitiated, gifting circles are tiny, grassroots, and community-focused informal organizations that were gaining popularity across North America at the time.

These kinds of informal groups operate under lots of different names. Sometimes, they're called a gifting circle, while other times, they're called a blessing loom or a susu. Whatever the name, you can think about it as a voluntary support system that helps build community and gives back to members. Some people think about it like a savings club. It's not an investment scheme, and it's not a pyramid scheme (although sometimes people do dress up traditional pyramid schemes with this kind of verbiage, which can lead to confusion.)

The whole thing works like this: participants voluntarily provide a gift to the circle; when a member's birthday rolls around, that member receives the amount available as a gift at that time. So, if eight members put in $5000, the person in the birthday seat would receive $40,000. And, traditionally, part of that $40,000 would go back in during the next round of giving. It was a great little financial boost for a single mother like myself; everyone I knew who participated was a completely normal, working, or middle-class person who stood to benefit from such a windfall. These weren't people looking for fast cash or to take advantage of others; these were regular, hard-working people who simply recognized the importance of financial well-being in our society.

Even before I became directly involved, I had seen firsthand these groups do so much good for so many people. I took the time to educate myself on whether this was legitimate or a scam. I'd never become involved in something I didn't think was on the up and up, but more importantly, I'd never share information about such a thing with others, either. To be clear, this wasn't any kind of investment scam, and it wasn't any kind of pyramid scheme where members were drawn in with promises to benefit those at the top. There was no hierarchy: this was a circle of members of the community getting together to work for our mutual benefit. As you might imagine, gifting circles are entirely legal. There is nothing remotely illegal about what I just described, *obviously*.

Look, I'm not naive. Maybe you read the description of the gifting circle and think, "That's a Ponzi. Maybe not technically, but the rest is semantics," and I totally respect that opinion (your feelings would be rooted in a misunderstanding, but I absolutely respect that others might feel differently than I.) You don't have to think that a gifting circle is a great thing to recognize the injustice of what was done to me (and others who would also be arrested.) Agree with participants or not, the members of this informal community were all adults, of sound mind. No one was enticed to participate; no one made false promises. Nobody lost money; it was the opposite. The people who participated benefited. But again, even if you think it's a bad thing, that's not the point. We might disagree about any number of things that other people do as consenting adults. If it's not illegal, and no one is being harmed, it seems a terrible waste of public resources to have police make bogus arrests that don't result in convictions. Especially when Canada has a serious organized crime problem, but I digress.

Canada's west coast can be a little temperamental in terms of weather in the winter months, but for the most part, it tends to be much milder and less snowy than the rest of the country. Think of it like much of the Pacific Northwest: we get lots of rain but not many days of freezing temperatures or snow. At the time, I was living in Maple Ridge, which is a beautiful little city in the lower mainland of British Columbia. As I recall, this January 9th was a pretty standard winter day in my neck of the woods. I mean — it *was* pretty standard, save for the fact that I, a law-abiding single mom, was stopped on the way to my speaking engagement and falsely arrested.

That evening I was bringing a friend to the presentation at a hotel in Coquitlam, which is about a half-hour drive from where I lived. In the mostly cooperative weather, we made what should have been an unremarkable drive to our destination. Now remember, I was *excited* to speak. I was wondering what the turnout would be like and thinking of everything I'd say – that is, when suddenly, I was jolted from those thoughts. I saw flashing lights in my rear view mirror, and then, they were beside me, too. *What was going on?* I was suddenly surrounded by what seemed like an entire motorcade of police cars signaling for me to pull over. I looked at my friend, both of us totally bewildered, and I decreased my speed. I flicked on the signal to indicate I was pulling over and slowly brought the car to a stop on the side of the road. After the car came to a stop I looked again at my friend. "I don't think I was speeding," I said, totally stunned at this bizarre turn of events.

A short, stocky, and terse woman approached my driver's side door. I had already rolled down my window, hoping more than anything to get some clarification as to what was going on. There were six police cars from what I could see. They had surrounded my car. This didn't seem like I was being pulled over for a traffic infraction. My mind raced, considering everything from there being something wrong with my car to something terrible happening to one of my children.

"Are you Chrystal Lee?" She asked.

"Yes," I stammered. Her asking my name like this only increased my fear and confusion. Clearly, they were looking for me. *But why?*

"Step out of the car for me, ma'am." She started to open my door as she finished her sentence. I hurriedly undid my seatbelt and immediately stepped out, hoping, more than anything, that some of this would start to make sense to me. Unfortunately, it only got worse from there.

"Chrystal Lee, I'm placing you under arrest for running an illegal lottery," she continued.

I think I let out a stunned gasp that was something between an incredulous laugh and an exclaim of pure shock.

"An *illegal lottery*? Wha- what?" I looked around at the other police officers, hoping for some kind of further clarification or information, but none would be forthcoming. I looked at my friend; our eyes locked for a moment of pure confusion. But there would be no further explanation. I was simply marched back to one of the cruisers, placed in handcuffs, and seated in the backseat of the car that would soon begin driving me to the police station. Before we left, they allowed my friend to drive my car home, which, at that moment, made me feel better. I was relieved that she would be okay and that my car wouldn't be towed or cause an accident or be left on the side of the highway. That feeling of relief wouldn't last long, however.

When you're sitting in the back of a police car, arrested for a crime you didn't commit, your mind tends to race. In one moment, I'd be calm and think, this is a mistake; this will all be sorted out soon. In the next, I'd be terrified. What would my children think? Was I going to jail right now? What was going to happen next?

I remember gathering myself in the moment and focusing intently on my kids. At that time, I had a 16-year-old and a 14-year-old, who were home babysitting their younger siblings, who were six and eight years old, for a couple of hours while I did my talk. But before I could drive myself too crazy thinking about my kids, we were back at the station.

Mercifully, they declined to place me in a holding cell and, instead, allowed me to sit on a bench while the process got started. That little act of kindness would be the last one I'd see from the police involved in handling this matter, but at the time, I didn't know that. I was grateful for that gesture, honestly. I waited there for what seemed like an eternity, but really, it was closer to a little over an hour. At that point, they stood me up and prepared to subject me to interrogation.

Right off the bat, I had the opportunity to speak to a lawyer. The person I spoke to advised me quite plainly that regardless of my guilt or innocence, I should not answer the police's questions and simply remain silent. I knew the lawyer was almost certainly an expert in what was happening here, and that their advice was probably correct; however, I also knew that I hadn't committed any crime. I wasn't a criminal. I was a single mom going to give a presentation on gifting, and then going home to her kids. *This had to be some sort of misunderstanding.*

After the call concluded, they brought me back to the interrogation room and asked me if I wanted to talk about what was going on – I immediately said yes, and that I wanted to explain everything. You have to remember that I knew that what I was doing was totally legal, and the illegal lottery charge convinced me that this was all just some kind of misunderstanding. Even though the lawyer advised me not to answer questions, I felt like if I could explain things, I was certain that they would see the truth, and this wouldn't go any further.

My chief interrogator was a male constable named Callahan. A short, thin-lipped man with beady eyes, he was as unimpressive physically as he was intellectually. He wasn't particularly unpleasant during my interrogation; he was just mostly devoid of any emotion or interest at all. His eyes were vacant. He seemed to vacillate between obvious disinterest and feigned curiosity. At the time, I just thought he was probably overworked, and maybe he even recognized how ridiculous this all was. I mean, let's get real here. You're arresting a single mother on a bogus charge that wouldn't have been particularly serious, even if it had any merit. This isn't exactly the crime of the century we're talking about. In any event, I have no way of knowing what he actually thought, and he did nothing outwardly to make me think he thought positively or negatively about me. Later, however, that would certainly change.

I was as open and honest with Callahan and the other officers as I could possibly be. Frankly, my need to explain myself wasn't just driven by the knowledge that I was innocent. I've always needed approval from people; it's part of my personality. We can speculate on the childhood traumas associated with this kind of need, and indeed, I'll write much about this in future chapters, but all of that aside, a great many of us are people pleasers. Those of us more inclined to this orientation are certainly more likely to want to explain ourselves, generally. This probably won't help you if you're being interrogated by the police. In my case, however, because the charges were wrongful to begin with, it probably did help. My lawyer commented something to this effect after he watched footage of my interrogation. Generally speaking, however, you probably shouldn't talk to the police if they suspect you of a crime, even if, like me, you happen to be completely innocent.

We spoke for more than an hour. I didn't just answer questions; I volunteered information. Hell, I practically did an entire presentation, complete with visual aids, on the entire topic. I was entirely forthright and honest. I wanted to turn these cops into experts on gifting circles. More than that, I made it explicit: I didn't think there was any kind of legal wrongdoing here whatsoever, but if I was wrong, and they could point to some law being broken, something I could assist them in stopping or preventing the future, well, I wanted to do just that. Up to this point, I'd never been involved in anything illegal or even somewhat sketchy my entire life – I certainly wasn't interested in starting a life of crime or running afoul of the police now. I was certain that I hadn't done anything remotely illegal or even untoward. Why wouldn't I be entirely forthright?

It's hard to say, but I think they were a little taken aback by my demeanor. It's my suspicion that police are probably used to the people they accuse of crimes of being a little more cagey and discriminating with the information they provide, but I was an open book. I wanted to help. I kept reiterating to them that I wanted to help in any way I could and that I thought that this was most likely just a misunderstanding.

At the time, I couldn't tell what they thought. The officers conducting my interrogation were totally humorless, mostly devoid of any emotion at all, and just clearly not interested in signaling to me what they thought, one way or the other. The interrogation concluded, and they started to process me.

I'm sure everyone is different, but in my case, it was during processing that the emotions of what I was experiencing actually started to hit me. They took my fingerprints and photographed me. I wanted to crawl into a hole and cry. It was embarrassing; it was humiliating. It made me feel ashamed, which, I would imagine, especially with hindsight, is essentially part of the goal of the arrest process. I finally couldn't hold back any longer, and I actually did start crying. I remember crying through my fingerprinting and crying through the mugshots. My crying actually messed up the fingerprinting process. I just couldn't believe that any of this was happening. I'd been working so hard and living what I felt was an honorable life. *Why was this happening?*

Finally, I was given the notice that I'd be able to call for someone to come pick me up, but by this point, they'd seized my phone as evidence, so I didn't have any of my phone numbers on me. The only number I could remember by heart was my mother's phone number, and for a variety of reasons, I really did not want to burden her with this. Without getting into too many of the details at this point in the story, while I had lived a totally straight-arrow life up to this point, the same couldn't be said for my brother. My mother had, more than a few times, been woken up by a phone call from someone at the police station in regard to some trouble my brother had found himself in. Between myself and my brother, I had always been the responsible child. I couldn't shatter that and get my mom involved in this.

I was thinking what I was going to do to get out of this and get home without shattering my mom's image of me when a police officer turned my way. "Hey, your boyfriend's outside." I was stunned. How did my boyfriend know about this? I suddenly felt a moment of relief, but – and you may be sensing a trend here – that wouldn't last long.

My boyfriend at the time, Shane, figured out pretty quickly that I had likely been arrested because he called home, and my daughter explained that the police had come and taken the car shortly after my friend had driven home with it and dropped it off. So, he figured – *no one can get in touch with her. She was supposed to be speaking at this event, but she didn't show up, and now the cops come and take her car. She must have been arrested.*

He started calling around police stations and when he reached Coquitlam, they affirmed that I was there. So, Shane was there to pick me up, and I, still completely bewildered and traumatized by the whole experience, left the police station without having to make a prohibitively long walk home. On the drive, Shane explained the sequence of events, and that's when it finally hit me – the police had seized my car. I didn't get it at first; why would they release the car with my friend and allow her to drop it off at my house? I eventually realized it was just something as banal as them not wanting to give my friend a ride home. So they let her drive it back to my place, knowing that they could just seize it later, which they did.

But this was just getting more and more confusing. I had just bought that car with no money down. Now, they were telling me they were seizing it as it was the proceeds of crime. *Are you guys taking over my payments?* I thought to myself. They did not, in fact, take over my payments.

I stood in my dining room at the time and, after relaying the entire embarrassing, horrible story to my oldest daughter, started to ponder as to just how I found myself in this position. Look, anyone can tell you that life tends to throw you curveballs. But a curveball is when your washing machine breaks or when you have a sudden and unexpected car-related expense. Getting falsely arrested is a little more than your standard, run-of-the-mill problem in life. But, like all things, it's not the event itself but the eventual fallout and consequences that would bring about the most change.

I felt that I wasn't rattled easily in life, but that night, I was rattled. Knowing that I was innocent wasn't enough; these people had the power to destroy my life. What had already happened was a massive disruption. My mind started to race. This wasn't just going to be stressful; this was going to be expensive, which was going to make everything else harder. At that moment, my eyes landed on a bottle of red wine sitting on the kitchen counter. I certainly drank before this event; heck, there was a bottle of red wine on my kitchen counter. Prior to my arrest, however, my alcohol consumption was limited to a few glasses of wine on the weekends, at the most. Or, maybe I'd have a glass of wine with a special dinner, especially with company involved. But that was the extent of my drinking before I was falsely arrested.

I need a drink, I thought. I didn't just want a drink; I needed one. And so I drank the entire bottle of wine. With hindsight, this was an obvious coping response to a traumatic event. Acknowledging the trauma and trying to talk through your feelings is a much healthier, more productive response likely to yield a positive outcome. But I didn't have that understanding then. And so I started drinking. Later, I would start abusing cocaine, as well. These substances would combine into powerful addictions that nearly destroyed my life.

But to really understand the story from here, we have to understand the root of addiction, and so we must go back to my childhood. In the following chapters, I'll take you through events in my life that have shaped me and ultimately set the stage for my addiction and recovery following my false arrest. To truly understand a person's addiction, we need to understand the root causes of their trauma and the reasons behind their feelings of shame. In my case, like with virtually all of us, it started in the family.

ONE: GETTING ARRESTED CHANGES YOUR LIFE

Two: Family Ties and Trauma

Regardless of our personal circumstances or situation, our early family lives are invariably laden with trauma. For the lucky among us, these are relatively benign forms of trauma that we heal from as we grow and develop as human beings. For those less fortunate, and in reality, that's probably most of us, our experiences can have indelible, lifelong impacts. In so many ways, I had a loving, happy, normal childhood. In other ways, my childhood was marked by disruption and trauma. My mom and dad did not have a healthy relationship, and they would divorce early on.

Before I get into the particulars of my familial relationships growing up, I feel the need to express that neither of my parents were supportive people. In fact, I often felt deliberately undermined by my parents. I'm not going to romanticize my parents or pretend that they were supportive or kind people who nurtured me. They did none of these things. I honestly believe that they were incapable as neither of them were there for me the way they should have been in my formative, developing years. However, after many years of working through my healing and looking back on our family life from a different perspective, I'm in a better position to understand how and why the various incidents took place. I don't blame any of my problems or the issues I've encountered in my life on my parents. I take responsibility for myself. I hold myself accountable for the decisions that I've made that turned out poorly. Now, I have a much more positive, healthy relationship with my mother. But that took a lot of time.

Many parents emotionally and physically abandon their children. There is a wide breadth of research showing that such kinds of abandonment represent an impactful form of trauma in a child's developing years and can lead to what the brilliant John Bradshaw and Dr. Gabor Maté refer to as toxic shame. This is an internalized sense of inferiority and shame that envelopes a person's entire sense of self. This stands in contrast to normal, healthy shame, which is an essential emotion felt by all human beings. Toxic shame is an all-encompassing sense that there is something inherently wrong with you. It stems directly from the trauma we experience as children whose parents abandon us.

I don't think either of my parents intended to inflict trauma upon me. That's the insidious nature of this kind of trauma – generational trauma – it is passed down unwittingly, and typically unknowingly, from parents to their children. In fact, there is evidence through our family history that both my mother and father were victims of abandonment within their own families.

My mother was the middle child of three children born in the Netherlands. It was a family affected by tragedy early on. My mother's brother, the younger of the three children and the first boy, died as an infant, and it was shortly thereafter that the family immigrated to Canada. It was right after the Second World War and they settled in the Prairies. Speaking very little English, my grandparents started to build a new life, having three more children born in Canada. I've never spoken in-depth with my mother about the degree to which she was affected by this tragedy growing up, but it would be impossible for such a tragedy not to affect family dynamics.

The family was mired with secrecy from the time that my grandparents immigrated from Holland. They didn't share much with us about their lives in Holland or their struggles and challenges having immigrated to a new country with very little, if any, support. But growing up, we were exposed to family secrecy, deception, physical abuse, adultery, alcoholism and drug addiction, to name a few. Our family was filled with jealousy, favoritism, sibling rivalry and overall, as the family grew, so did the familial issues.

My mother once shared with us children that when she was a young girl of only eight years old, she contracted Scarlet Fever and was hospitalized for almost six months. She shared with us that during her hospital stay, she didn't receive any visitors; neither her parents nor her siblings came to visit her. This sense of abandonment definitely left a profoundly deep wound, and understandably would be traumatizing for any child. To this day, she still suffers from lingering effects of Scarlet Fever, and the effects of feeling abandoned as a child have had devastating effects on her relationships.

When my mother was a young woman of only 18 years old, she met a young man of the same age who was attending university to become a meteorologist. My mother had been accepted to nursing school and soon found herself studying to become a nurse at a college in Manitoba. It was during their youthful courtship that my mother became pregnant – something that was very frowned upon in those days. Women weren't just shunned for youthful pregnancies, they often got ostracized from their family and friends. This type of act would be devastating to every facet of their lives. More than that, her parents, my grandparents, were devout Roman Catholics and therefore, very strict parents. This affair would potentially have devastating consequences and be looked down upon by the community, most importantly, by the family. My mother decided to quit her nursing education and bravely returned home to confide in her parents about becoming pregnant. She was terrified to share the news with them for fear of destroying the family name and pride. Their response was much the same as other parents' during that era – they had to get married. So, at the ripe young age of only 19 years old, my mother found herself at the altar, marrying her young boyfriend, and shortly thereafter, my sister was born.

Today, I really relate to the decisions my mother made as a young woman, especially those she made in fear. She did what she thought was best, it maintained the family, at least for a time. She would have faced a tremendous amount of internal and external pressure to have the child on her own. Still, we can only lie to ourselves for so long before the effects begin to show.

Unfortunately, the marriage was doomed from the start. Two young adults of only 19 years old, pressured into marriage and with a newborn was difficult in those times, to say the least. My mother's new husband was still in university and was rarely home. For practical reasons, their life together didn't last very long, and they divorced a couple of years later. By that time, my grandparents had moved the rest of the family to the west coast. My mother, now a single young woman with an infant, decided to take my sister and move out west to be with the rest of her family.

It was a couple of years later when my mother was working at a local department store that she met my father. My mother was incredibly beautiful, especially when she was younger. She was tall and slender, looked like Audrey Hepburn and attracted a lot of attention because of her physical beauty. That's probably a big reason why my dad was with her because they didn't have much else in common. My dad never wanted children, and he already had a child with another woman, with whom he didn't have much of a relationship. Nonetheless, when my mother became pregnant with me, they married and started a life together. It was just eighteen months later that my mother became pregnant again and had my brother.

In hindsight, I can say that my mother was terribly affected by mental health issues. Her youth was difficult. Her parents, my grandparents, were very strict, and being the second child with three younger brothers, she was made responsible for much of the work around the house. She was surrounded by strong, masculine men and was exposed to much of their aggression. She didn't have a very close relationship with her mother and rarely saw her sister. As an adult, she was officially diagnosed with borderline personality disorder (BPD), which can be an extremely debilitating condition. People with BPD engage in all types of negative behaviors that harm their interpersonal relationships. Moreover, while she's never been officially diagnosed, and while I'm certainly no clinician, it wouldn't surprise me to learn she has narcissistic personality disorder (NPD) as well. She's a textbook narcissist. I find I can better understand her behaviors when I consider that she's living with very real ailments that affect her ability to relate to people.

Six months after my brother was born, my father walked out on us. My mother inevitably had a nervous breakdown. Again, I try to look back with empathy. My father wasn't a particularly loving or supportive person. My mother, only twenty-seven years old, was now a single mother with three small children and didn't have much in terms of either practical help or emotional support. Her inability to care for herself, let alone her children, was when my sister, only eight years old at the time, had to step up and become a surrogate mother. My mom's breakdown was the beginning of the end – everything remotely normal in our lives started to fall apart. My mother was devastated to find out that my father left her for another woman, who would eventually become his next wife. That was the end of my mother and father's marriage and the beginning of our horror. I saw my father intermittently after the breakup, on weekends and holidays when we would visit with him and his new family. We did maintain a relationship, and later as a young teenager, I'd live with him for a time.

Even as a child, I could understand my parents' separation, especially from my dad's perspective. My mother could be a very difficult woman, and it wasn't hard to understand why anyone would want to distance themself from many of her behaviors. Even today, while our relationship is much better than when I was young, she remains difficult. I used to be embarrassed when I'd go out with her because invariably, she'd be rude to someone or do or say something totally out of bounds. She hasn't really changed, to be honest, but today, we have a much more healthy and loving relationship. She's obviously learned from some of her mistakes, and my ability to set boundaries as an adult has helped a lot.

My mom, newly single and very distraught from the marriage breakup, struggled to maintain our household with three small children of eight and two years old and a six-month old infant. For a few years after my father left, my mother remained single and tried to get back on her feet after the nervous breakdown. When she did start to pull her life together, she started going out more and my sister was tasked with babysitting and caring for us. However, if my sister was unavailable to babysit, my mother would often ask the neighbour, Bonnie, to watch over us. Bonnie was a teenager who lived next door with her parents and two younger brothers. I was around four or five years old at the time, so when she would come to babysit my brother and me, we would play together or read or watch television shows – all the normal things young children would do at that age. However, over time, things gradually became perverse… I recall several occasions when Bonnie made advances on both my brother and me. She kissed me on the lips; she kissed my brother, who was eighteen months younger than me, on the lips. Her advances progressed to cataglottism – kissing us with her tongue - and touching our young bodies. I sensed it was wrong, but at that age and time, I was terrified to tell anyone. We were both terrified of the possible consequences. This behavior carried on for a couple of years, until the time that Bonnie and her family moved away. To this day, I have only shared this experience with my counsellors. Looking back, it's understandable how yet another form of abuse had played a part in my addictions, as well as my brother's, adding to further shame and secrecy about what happened.

Our household was often filled with yelling and screaming and constant hostility and a chaotic whirlwind of disruption and insecurity filled my being. Honestly, those experiences are an important part of who I have become; I'm a fighter. I'm kind – I don't want to fight with anyone. But I also won't back down from a fight. I had to learn to protect myself during times of great hostility, chaos, and unpredictability, and this ability to fight has helped me to overcome great challenges in life, including my addiction. Over the years, my life growing up in a chaotic, unsettling, and unpredictable environment, was something that I became so accustomed to and familiar with, that as a young adult, life did not seem normal unless there was some chaotic or dramatic event that was taking place. Hence the start of my dopamine addiction.

It was around this same period of time that my mother met a young man, named Bob Smith. Bob was seven years her junior. He was a tall, very strong and muscular young man, with a ginger complexion and a full head of hair. He had a beard and mustache and wore metal-rimmed glasses. Things happened quickly between my mother and Bob, and he gradually became a constant presence in my life from the time that I was four or five years old until I was almost twelve. We often went out on weekends to the beach or to a park, and during the summer we'd sometimes go camping. He had started staying over at our house more regularly, and eventually he and my mom bought a house together, which was only possible because my mom sold our house and used the proceeds. Now that they were living together, Bob had become more like a stepfather figure to me during those formative years of my childhood.

Bob was an extremely abusive man. He had a terrible temper; there was no in-between with Bob. Most of the time, he was exceptionally calm and even keeled, but when he became angry, it was an onslaught of rage, yelling, and physical violence. Looking back on this violence, he was extremely passive-aggressive, switching between a shy sense of calm one second and rage the next. His behavior became unpredictable, and we were all terrified of him. Bob would mercilessly abuse my mother, focusing his rage as expressions of physical abuse against her. As horrible as it was, it was made even worse by the fact that this violence would occur directly in front of us children.

One such event occurred when I was only nine years old, and we all went to California on vacation. It was going to be a great time and our very first trip to California, with plans to visit Disneyland and San Diego. I was so excited! We drove down in Bob's truck – my mom, sister, brother, Bob, and his sister. We made it to San Diego in under twenty hours, driving non-stop. We visited Magic Mountain and even went across the border into Tijuana, Mexico. One day, while staying at a motel in San Diego, a fight broke out between Bob and my mother. Bob hauled off and hit my mother, swinging wildly with brute force.

My mom, no match for Bob's strength, went flying into the corner of a dresser. It was a startling explosion of rage, and it happened right in front of us kids. My mom was bruised from the waist down both sides of her hips and legs. My sister quickly ushered my brother and I out of that motel room – the three of us walking aimlessly in a daze and in shock for what we had just witnessed. I have no idea why or how the fight started and all I remember afterwards is that we hurriedly packed up, were ushered into the truck, and we made our way back home, cutting our trip short.

Sadly, it wasn't just my mom who was the focus of Bob's violence. I can remember both my sister and my brother being violently abused by Bob. Searching my memory, I know I was also the target of his abuse, but it was mostly my brother and sister being more frequent targets of his rage. Whether it was because my sister was older and thus more likely to do something to draw his ire by protecting us and stepping in to stop him from beating us, or because my brother was a boy, living with three women, and he had to be "toughened up," I do not know. The amount of violence in the household between the man positioned as my stepfather and my mother was nothing short of soul-crushing for a young child.

I recall one such incident when I was on the receiving end of his abuse – I was all but five years old. My sister had given me three white porcelain poodles as a Christmas gift. They were only a few inches tall, each one with a black collar and connected to each other by a tiny gold chain leash. To me, they were special. They represented my big sister, me, and my little brother. I loved those poodles so much that I placed them on my windowsill in my bedroom, where I could see them as I closed my eyes before going to sleep. One night, as it was my time to go to sleep, Bob came into my room to close the blinds. As he did so, he knocked over my porcelain poodles. They fell to the floor, smashing into tiny pieces - destroyed. I screamed in horror that he broke my poodles and cried aloud hysterically. It was a deep, guttural cry, tears streaming down my face as I saw my poodles shattered into tiny pieces all over the floor. Bob wasn't pleased with my reaction and didn't offer an apology. Grabbing me by my arm he swung me around and proceeded to spank me repeatedly on my behind. I screamed out in pain; struggling to get away from him only made things worse. Those beady eyes hiding behind his rimmed glasses held nothing but contempt and anger. There was no understanding or compassion for a little girl who had just lost her prize memento – he showed no remorse whatsoever. He was cold and in a rage. Besides the bruises I was left with on my arm and my behind and the sadness and pain that I felt both physically and emotionally, I was riddled with confusion. Why was I getting punished when it was him that broke my poodles? I couldn't understand. All I knew was from that day onwards, that same pain and sadness is what I feel today when I am deeply saddened and troubled. I recognize that pain all too well.

To further complicate things, my mom was also physically and emotionally abusive. Having to defend herself and protect herself from this monster was difficult, and unfortunately, the rage was then passed on to us children. She suffered from her own addictions; while she never had a penchant for alcohol, growing up I became more and more aware that she regularly took a variety of pills. While we children weren't just the targets of Bob's abuse; indeed, we got it from my mother, too.

Eventually, their relationship ended. It was one summer weekend when my mother went away to a retreat. She knew the relationship was falling apart and needed a respite to clear her head. My brother and I stayed with our grandparents that weekend, and my sister stayed at the house because she was then working. Bob was supposed to pick up my mother from the retreat on Sunday afternoon, but never showed up. Somehow, my mother was able to pick up my brother and I, and we went home to find our house completely empty! Bob had taken everything. It was the perfect crime – one year to the day of them living together in the new house. He took our beds, the living room and kitchen furniture - everything that we had brought from our old house – it was all gone. He left us with nothing. This was the ultimate act of betrayal, which left us impoverished and devastated my mother both emotionally and financially. I don't think she has ever fully recovered or healed from that incident and what that man did to our lives.

We had to sell the house because alone, my mother couldn't afford it. We moved into a little duplex, and my sister went backpacking in Europe for six months. When she returned, she had to live with our maternal grandparents, primarily because there wasn't enough room in the small house for all of us. I think this became a deep regret for my mom; having sold our house to move in with Bob. It cost her half of the equity she had in our house, and I'm sure it cost her so much more. I've never pressed for details, but it's obvious to me that that relationship has been a longstanding regret of hers. In many ways, I don't think she ever recovered from what that man did to us. He was a monster. Over the years, my mother dated a couple of men, but her trauma and fear always got the best of her. My mother has been single for approximately twenty-five years now, with no interest in pursuing a romantic relationship. Her focus changed after that tragedy, to be on my brother, who started using drugs. He, too, couldn't get over the abuse he suffered at the hands of Bob. My brother was tortured emotionally and physically by the man that he looked up to as a small boy. Having Bob in our household, and in our lives affected each one of us differently, and for me, I was deeply affected by his unpredictable rage.

I have struggled with my emotional intelligence throughout my life, and I think part of that relates to me having inherited some of my negative behaviors and patterns from my mom. This is something that I work on because it's important to me that I do not repeat negative patterns or behaviors and that I overcome negative models to which I was exposed throughout my childhood.

I have a lot of empathy for my mother. Later in this book I will talk a little more about our current relationship and how grateful I am to still be connected to her. The kinds of pain and trauma that we've experienced have absolutely ruptured close relationships. She is not perfect, but she is not a monster. She did the best she could, and in my own journey toward recovery, the insights and learning I've gained have truly helped me to see her in a new light and better understand why she behaved the way she did.

When I was 14 years old, I left my mom's house and moved in with my dad, who by now had a new wife with kids and was living on Vancouver Island. Prior to my moving in with him, we had visited with him intermittently on weekends, birthdays and holidays. I never really fit in with his new family because, from my dad's perspective, I was tainted. Neither of my parents had particularly healthy or constructive views on their post-divorce relationship. I had to listen to each one badmouth the other and I was often interrogated by my mother about visits with my father. I always felt that I was treated with indifference by my father, mostly because he hated my mom.

Despite all of this, over the years, my father and I had maintained a relatively decent relationship; we stayed in touch. We weren't close, but we did have a relationship. I always made sure to include him and his new wife in all of our family gatherings and children's birthdays. One thing would change all of that, however, my arrest. His reaction was bizarre; you'd think I was arrested for and guilty of crimes against humanity. He cut me off and refused to even acknowledge my existence afterward. It feels absurd to even write; I was arrested (and ultimately exonerated) years ago. He still pretends I'm dead, like my being arrested sullied his good name irrevocably.

I can imagine for some, having their child get arrested would be shameful; however, never speaking to them again, nor attempting to fully understand the reason for the arrest, is incomprehensible to me. But that was his decision. I stopped feeling bad about it a while ago, even if I've never really understood it. I can't torture myself trying to understand the motivation behind what is rationally inexplicable behavior. It's such a cliche, but what else can be said? It is what it is.

Today, my father has no relationship with any of his adult children related by blood. He didn't show up to my brother's funeral, leaving me with a sense of his indifference and general abandonment of us kids. He does, however, have a relationship with my older sister, with whom he is not biologically related. I have never been able to fully understand this, and it is only my father who can shed light upon this indifference, yet he chooses to remain silent. It has left me to ponder whether his deep-seated resentment and dislike for my mother is also what has caused him to distance himself from me. He has never tried to make me feel otherwise. It's hard for me to wrap my head around, but that's the most sense I can make of it.

It could also be that he feels terrible guilt and shame over his abandonment of his biological children. Seeing us or interacting with us reminds him of his failures. As a result, it's probably much easier for him to pretend we don't exist. Otherwise, on some level, he'd have to confront his failures and come to terms with his life as it has turned out. My need to rationalize and understand the situation, admittedly, is a form of making assumptions and has been the only way that I have been able to come to terms with his behavior. He recently got divorced and now lives alone. It's not really the most surprising outcome for the kind of man I just described.

In stark contrast to my father, my sister is not only brilliant but has tremendous emotional intelligence. She came to me recently and confided that she was concerned that even maintaining a relationship with him was like a betrayal to me. She is very insightful, and she recognized that it could be the kind of thing that hurt my feelings. Her even having awareness of that possibility really highlights how fortunate I am to have her in my life. All of us act thoughtlessly at times, even when we mean well; she's always acted thoughtfully, and for her, I am eternally grateful.

As an adult, especially one who's experienced addiction and recovery, I have an acute awareness of the role that shame plays, both in fueling addiction as well as inhibiting recovery. Much has been written on the topics of shame and addiction, and I won't rehash it all here. Still, I will say that certain authors like Dr. Gabor Maté and John Bradshaw have done remarkable work on helping to promote understanding with respect to the links between shame, addiction, and childhood trauma. The work of Bradshaw and, indeed, a great many others in this area makes clear the connections between emotional abandonment in childhood and the development of shame and addiction. It becomes a vicious cycle where shame reinforces addiction, and then addiction reinforces shame. Just recognizing the role that our own childhood traumas play in these behaviors can be empowering and help you to break the cycle.

Certainly, both my parents emotionally abandoned me, as they did with my brother and sister. It wasn't malicious; they probably weren't trying to cause us shame or trauma, but it would be foolish to pretend otherwise. When we are honest with ourselves about how our parents let us down, we can begin to recognize how to change our thinking about certain aspects of ourselves and our lives. This isn't about de-monizing our parents or shifting responsibility for things that have gone wrong in our lives; our parents are human and there is no manual on how to be a good parent. When we recognize that they, too, had to learn and grow along the way, we can better recognize our own human-ity. In doing so, we create the space needed to allow our own growth and healing to occur. And, as I can personally attest, nothing helps promote forgiveness like feeling as though you are living authentically and honoring yourself. Even today, I don't carry anger for my father or my mother. I love my mother. I see her as a flawed but good human being. As for my father, I feel mostly indifference. I don't think about him much and I certainly don't carry any ill will toward him.

Three: Realizing a Dream

So many things, from familial pressure to cultural norms, tell us we must get married and have a family when we come of age. The thing about cultural norms is that they become ingrained in all of us; our genuine wants reflect these norms. I'm not sure if it was all the movies and stories I consumed growing up or if it's always been a part of me, but I genuinely wanted to fall in love, get married, and have children. The idea of having a family always represented an ideal life, the best of what life could offer. After all, what could be better than bringing children into this world, loving them, and raising them to be good, hard-working people who themselves would contribute to the betterment of the world? For me, there was nothing else. I even had a clear idea in my head of the age I'd meet my husband, when I'd get married, when I'd have my first child, and so on. It wasn't some kind of rigid schedule to which I had to adhere; it was just a clear idea in my mind about my life and how it would unfold.

Having grown up in a very religious Roman Catholic family, we regularly attended church on Sundays and catechism on Wednesday evenings, that was, at least, until Bob and my mom split up. After Bob left, we stopped attending church altogether. I remember that I was in grade seven at the time. Many things had changed at home, we were in a different house and my sister was no longer living with us. Attending church became much less of a priority for my mom. She had other things to deal with and worry about. I wouldn't say that I was especially disillusioned with faith at the time, but I was entering an increasingly rebellious and independent time of youth. I stopped engaging with my religious or spiritual sides, for the most part, at least for the next several years. It wouldn't be until I was an adult that I'd reconnect with my faith more fully and more meaningfully.

When I was 26, I gave my heart to Jesus. I was attending an Alpha Program, which for the unfamiliar, is a ten-week program designed to help participants explore Christianity in a non-denominational setting. The idea is basically to create a safe space where people can explore their relationship with Jesus and develop connections with others in a supportive environment. At the close of the program, participants affirm their personal commitment to the Lord, a life of evangelization, and ultimately living a life consistent with the teachings of Christianity. As a young woman it was a lovely opportunity to connect more deeply with my spiritual side.

At the time I attended the program, I was in a relationship with a young man, who did not share my newfound spiritual awakening. It became clear that the relationship wouldn't continue to work. There was no animosity, but we made the mutual decision to go our separate ways. I think back on it today, and the maturity with which we both handled the situation was commendable.

So, I found myself single, with this newfound spiritual awakening. At the time, personal growth was becoming increasingly important to me, and roughly six months down the road, I attended a seminar on self-reflection and discovery. This was where I'd meet my future husband, Christopher.

It's important to understand that my religious and spiritual awakening became intertwined with falling in love with Chris. This context is especially important, not just for understanding our relationship, but the fallout I've endured and continue to endure. What's more, we had a true whirlwind romance. We became serious very quickly. Have you ever heard the term "love-bombed"? Chris love-bombed me, and it worked. Here was a man who apparently was fulfilling all my needs and desires in a romantic partner. I was over the moon!

I met Christopher on September 9, 2000, and we were married just a few short months later. Meeting Chris was such a whirlwind; it's hard to describe. Anyone who has quickly fallen in love would probably relate. But every situation is different, so I'll do my best to help you understand what our courtship was like because understanding my relationship with Chris is critically important for understanding my situation after our eventual divorce, as well as my struggles with addiction later in life.

Chris was also attending the seminar that weekend, and so we met in the context of this lovely gathering for self-reflection, personal empowerment, and growth. It was truly a positive atmosphere. What's more, Chris seemed to be attuned to faith in all the same ways I was becoming. It seemed as though our encounter was destiny. With hindsight, the truth is actually incredibly ugly; religion and my faith were used against me, to manipulate me. I'm not sure if he did these things deliberately and with malice, or if he was just completely disillusioned and lying to himself at the time.

In any event, our relationship blossomed very quickly; early on, he seemed to be completely in love with me and willing to do anything to sweep me off my feet. In reality he was manipulating and gaslighting me. I only realized later that one of the reasons I fell so hard for Chris was his manipulation and gaslighting techniques were very familiar to me. In many ways, this behavior mirrored what I received from my parents growing up.

It's important to keep in mind that I had a very traumatic childhood. Because of this, I had a really idealized concept of marriage in my mind. That might sound counterintuitive but the way in which I saw marriage – my own marriage, as an adult – was a kind of salvation to take me away from the trauma and hurt that I had experienced in my own family growing up. So, my expectations of marriage weren't very realistic, which was identified during the pre-marriage counselling provided through our church. The counsellor explained that I had a very idealized view of marriage, while Chris was extremely enmeshed with his own family. This enmeshment was something that could put him at odds with me. At the time, I had no idea how prescient that would be.

Later in life, I would be exposed to the wonderful work of Harville Hendrix and his wife, Helen LaKelly Hunt. They authored the seminal "Getting the Love You Want," a lovely and empowering book designed to help couples overcome their difficulties and foster a loving, conscious relationship. Hendrix and Hunt argue that many people enter into romantic relationships with unrealistic expectations. We expect our partner to innately understand us, as well as fill in the pieces of us that are missing, largely due to childhood traumas. This helped me to understand why I expected so much from my marriage and why I was ultimately disappointed. Our romantic partners cannot inherently heal our childhood traumas merely through their presence. With work and commitment, however, couples can communicate and reach a conscious state in their relationship, leading to a harmonious and beautiful union.

Unfortunately, my partner was neither attuned to these ideas nor interested in maintaining basic honesty, let alone interested in having a meaningful commitment. He was, however, interested in manipulating me to gain my compliance and trust. Christopher explained to me that he had had a vision from God, who explained to him that it was his destiny to meet and marry a woman named Chrystal. He went on to share this vision with friends and family with great exuberance. It was only three weeks later that he and I met at the weekend conference. He was so excited and convinced that I was brought into his life by the divine power of God that he didn't waste any time proposing to me. Whether he even had the vision or not, I have no idea; he had lied about so much. After much reflection, however, my suspicion is that it was a form of manipulation to draw me in. Later in our marriage, he would actually use the story of his vision to say some horribly disgusting things to our children, one of them being that he married the wrong "Chrystal." Imagine, as a child, hearing one of your parents say to you that being with the other parent was a mistake. The inference is clear that the child is then a mistake. It's an awful thing to even think, let alone to say to your children. I've always maintained that as bad as my relationship with Chris was, I would never regret the relationship because of my incredible children. To this day, I don't think he has the insight or awareness to make these connections. It's deeply troubling to me.

At the time, however, I really fell for him. I was young and naïve and had no comprehension nor awareness of the manipulation and deceit I would soon come to experience. He hadn't been transparent with me and was obviously hiding some deeply disturbing character flaws. He had only shown me a very small part of his personality – the part he wanted me to see – the friendly, bubbly and charismatic sides of Chris. Moreover, my journey of self-reflection and discovery was really just getting started. At that time, all I knew was that I had found a man that seemed to adore me and who apparently shared my connection to faith and a desire to have a committed and loving relationship. I was completely swept off my feet.

Chris and I decided to wait to consummate our relationship until we got married. We enjoyed spending time together, getting to know one another, but we didn't have sex until our wedding night, just three short months after meeting one another. Our delaying this intimacy was in keeping with our religious beliefs, but it also served to keep me in the dark about a number of important things in his life. These weren't minor things. I'm talking about fundamental aspects about who he was – and is – as a man.

During our courtship, I was completely unaware and would later learn that Chris came with some baggage. I slowly realized that he wasn't entirely who he had presented himself to be. Chris was very complex, and his unique experiences made him the charismatic person he was. Heck, that's why I was initially attracted to him. Chris had had a really wild and adventurous life before we met and before he committed himself to lead a life aligned with his religious values. Believe it or not, Chris fronted a relatively successful rock band that played the touring circuit with all the big bands of that time. So even though his band wasn't a household name, and never saw major success, he had been exposed to a very fast paced rockstar lifestyle for a significant part of his youth. Ask anyone you know who's had even minor, fleeting success in the music business - things can get more than a little crazy. Touring and playing shows, especially when you're young, is a recipe for wild times. There is a reason that sex, drugs, and rock-and-roll are synonymous with each other. I think these experiences played an important role in Christopher's addictions which would later come to wreak havoc on our marriage and home life.

Waiting to have sex until our wedding night was an important part of my devotion to starting a life with my new husband. It was difficult, that was for sure. But my opinion of sex at that time was that sex, especially in the context of a committed, loving relationship, is a beautiful thing between husband and wife and that all of us should be so fortunate to enjoy (and on a regular basis, at that!) I only bring this up because I had resolved in my mind that Chris' past was in the past and hearing about his promiscuous lifestyle didn't bother me because it was in the past. What mattered most was that we had made vows to each other in front of God. We were committed to each other in a sacred covenant.

Almost immediately after we got married, however, I recognized that something was amiss with the physical intimacy of our relationship. I didn't feel wanted or desired the way I had felt with other partners in my past. Being as honest as I can be, I certainly wasn't a virgin when I married Chris, but I didn't have a highly promiscuous past. Still, I knew enough to know that it could be better than this. It should be better than this, I thought. The only reason we did have sex was because I initiated sex. I'm a physical person. I think it's normal and healthy for two people in love to express their love physically. After all, sexual intimacy acts as a glue that bonds a couple together. But sometimes, with serious intimacy issues and other issues related to sexuality, like in Chris' case, sexual intimacy can be challenging.

Have you ever known someone deeply religious, or at least someone for whom religion and religious norms play a significant role in their life? In that case, you'll know that they can be deeply troubled by the rift between their own behavior and the standard they feel their behavior should meet. I believe Christopher was very much in this situation. Whether he felt genuine religious conviction or merely social and cultural pressures to conform to particular ideals and standards, I don't know (but I honestly do suspect that it is the latter rather than the former.) Regardless, Chris was a deeply conflicted man. He was married to me, which allowed him to feel as though he was living the kind of life he should have been living, according to his faith and family expectations. Under the surface, however, things were not what they seemed.

It was only about three weeks into our marriage, when the first bombshell dropped. It was a regular day in our new life together. I was sitting at the kitchen table, going through the mail, which included our monthly phone bill. A monthly bill was normally around $45, as I recall, so you might imagine that I was astounded when I opened the bill to find a balance of well over $500! It took me a moment to process. What the hell? I thought.

Thinking the number next to "balance owing" must be some kind of mistake, I started frantically opening the voluminous bill to see just where in the hell these charges were coming from. What could possibly explain such a high bill? In a moment, I'd have my answer. My eyes settled on one of the numbers listed in the log, which read something to the effect of: 1-900-SEX-6969. My heart sank. I frantically read through the bill and saw a series of substantial charges from numerous 1-900 lines. My husband of just a few weeks had racked up a bill of over $500 for phone sex! At first, I was stunned, my mind racing in shock. I didn't know what to think. On the one hand, I wanted to understand where my husband was coming from; on the other hand, I was filled with so many emotions. I was angry, ashamed, astonished, disgusted, and bewildered. Did he not realize that he'd get caught?!

Chris did his best to explain the charges, but you really can't explain $500 worth of phone sex charges any way other than, "I spent $500 on phone sex." There's no world where that could plausibly be an accident or for some innocent purpose. Were you doing hours of phone sex for research? Is this for an academic study I don't know about? Obviously, there are no answers to these questions because the whole situation is relatively straight forward: my new husband, who barely demonstrated any interest in sex with his new wife, was addicted to phone sex with God-knows-who. When I confronted him with the bill, he flatly, with no emotion in his voice, conceded that he had incurred the charges, saying, "By the way, I'm addicted to phone sex." With hindsight, I'm amazed at the restraint that I showed when in fact, I was enraged.

When you're in a really difficult situation with someone you love, your mind will do all kinds of incredible mental gymnastics to justify or rationalize the situation in which you find yourself. In my case, I found myself saying, "Well, it's not like he's sleeping with other people. I guess I can be thankful for that." But I wasn't thankful - I was mortified. This wasn't at all what I signed up for. And on this very normal day of my new married life, I was jolted to the realization that Chris was not at all who he proclaimed to be. These weren't minor character flaws; I came to realize that he had been lying about many things in his life. Eventually, I came to feel so bitter because I felt like I had been lured into the marriage under false pretenses, which would have made the covenant before God, null and void; I had been completely deceived. I remember crying, sobbing in a mixture of sadness and rage. My mind wandered, wondering if it was possible to get the marriage annulled.

As you might imagine, phone sex was just the start of my new husband's disgusting behavior. For the next three years - the first three years of our marriage – I made what amounted to weekly discoveries about Chris. It started with the phone sex, but it definitely didn't end there. One day, when I was confronted with information that he was spending a significant amount of money on pornography, I realized that he wasn't looking at normal, run-of-the-mill porn for straight guys. He was looking at hardcore gay porn. My husband didn't just have some minor issues around sex, he was closeted. At a minimum, he was bisexual. I struggled to comprehend his obviously bizarre and underhanded behavior in contrast with the things he said and did, gaslighting me constantly. He regularly rationalized his behavior stating, "At least I haven't fucked anyone – so therefore it's not considered cheating." He'd then say that since he had confessed his "sins" to me, that I had to forgive him 70 times seven times (in other words, infinitely), as it states in the Bible. So, I was not only being emotionally and physically abused, I later learned that this was a form of spiritual abuse.

Things were awful at home, but the saving grace, at that time, was my work. I was a tour guide for the Rocky Mountaineer railway traveling through the Rocky Mountains between British Columbia and Alberta. It was a very fun and positive work environment. In part, it was so enjoyable because of a lovely guy I worked with, Paul. When we were together at work everything about my life seemed normal again. We made each other laugh. I'd live in the moment, feeling a real human connection again. I felt whole again; happy and shielded from the hurt and betrayal that characterized my feelings toward Chris. It was so easy to forget about my husband, who was deceptive, emotionally distant, and interested in sex with anyone other than me. At home, I couldn't pretend reality wasn't what it was. I started to live a double life – vacillating from a life of hurt, pain, and betrayal to a life filled with joy, happiness, and acceptance.

Chris and I married on December 30, 2000. Paul and I had started working together around that time. We didn't get together, however, until 2003. So, we spent a good chunk of time just working together as platonic friends. Mind you, I almost immediately discovered Christopher's issues. I found the first astronomical phone bill just about a month after we got married. I didn't just start cheating with Paul; I suffered with Christopher's behavior for almost three years before Paul and I first started a romantic relationship.

We were still married, but I had moved out. I told Christopher I didn't want any part of his lies any longer and that I was going to be with Paul. At the time, we lived in Kelowna, and I worked out of Vancouver. I would come home to watch Erica, our daughter, on my days off and be with Paul while I was away working. Paul was his usual self, he was incredibly supportive and loving during this time, a time when I - obviously - was under a lot of stress.

I quickly came to realize that Christopher had a terrifying power over me. I increasingly became afraid that he'd use our new baby against me. At the time, our daughter, Erica, was just one year old.

Being physically separated from her wasn't just emotionally taxing, it caused me real practical fear.

Christopher had demonstrated that he was totally divorced from reality. Outwardly, he portrayed himself as a righteous and good man, a loving husband and father, who had been wronged by a crazy woman who had just left him. However, the reality was that Christopher was lying to everyone, including himself. I remember thinking what will he do? I was terrified. I feared that he would somehow use our young child to threaten me. The bond and love I had for my young child was like nothing I had experienced before. At times, Christopher made subtle threats about what he'd do if I didn't come home. At other times, he'd speak in grand metaphors, convinced he was being subtle, but it was anything but – it was painfully obvious what he was saying that he'd do if I didn't come home. He was going to do anything and everything he could to keep me under his control – including using my new daughter as a weapon against me. I was filled with fear.

Eventually, Chris was able to wear me down and convince me to come home. He was a master manipulator, and as such, he was very good at playing on my fears. He made me think I could lose custody of my daughter by threatening me with the law. He didn't just play on my deep-seated traumas; he filled my head with lies about what he'd do to gain custody of our baby and that I'd lose all access to her.

Paul saw clearly what was happening. He urged me not to go back to such a bad situation and that I'd be putting myself at terrible risk. At the time, however, I did still have some love for Chris and I felt terrible guilt and anxiety about a potential divorce. I remember distinctly hearing my father's mocking voice in my head: "You're going to wind up pregnant and divorced by the time you're 20, just like your mother." Those words have haunted my being since I was a young teenager at a critically important stage of my development. I was terrified that it would come to pass, and the fear and shame paralyzed me. This deep-seated trauma was a major factor in my return to my toxic and obviously unworkable marriage.

To make matters worse, Christopher's family, his church community, and even some of my own family seemed to side with him. At once, I was urged to overlook his obvious infidelity while shamed for my desire to be in a healthy relationship. What's more, I wanted to forgive Chris, if possible. If not for me, for our new child. I rationalized things; then, I only knew about his indiscretions over the phone and the porn addiction. While looking back, I have no idea what he was truly up to; at the time, I was still fairly naive. My heart was with Paul, but for whatever reason, I left him and went back with Chris. I think it was my belief in fantasy and my failure to see things as they truly were. That, of course, coupled with the threats, and obviously my deep-seated shame, which was being actively heightened by comments made by many of those who were supposed to be closest to me. Everyone in his family urged me to just get back with him. It seemed like I had every reason to go back.

Paul was devastated and understandably disapproving of my getting back with my abusive husband; Paul knew what Chris had put me through. Paul truly loved me, and he was crushed about my decision to go back. I still carry a lot of sadness and regret about having hurt him. Little did I know at the time, however, that my story with Paul wasn't over yet. But for now, I was a committed wife and mother. Even in the face of my husband's grotesque betrayal, I was willing to try to forgive for the sake of my family and my vows. I hadn't signed up for this; I signed up for a loving, normal marriage. But I was prepared to do anything I could to save the marriage, especially due to the external pressures heaped upon me and, of course, the shame stemming from my childhood.

Four: The Dream is Shattered

I had moved back in with Chris, but things still didn't sit right with me. Within three months, I was pregnant again with my second daughter, Annabelle. Right after her birth, I developed a terrible case of mastitis. If you don't know, that's an infection in your breast tissue. I had an awful fever and left Chris to take care of the little ones while I went to the hospital to get some antibiotics. After waiting and being in pain all night, I finally got the antibiotics and came home in a taxi. As I approached the house, I noticed that the living room light was on. I quietly walked up to the house and peeked in the window. There was my husband, sitting at the desk, watching gay porn on the computer. My heart sank. I knew then and there that I had made a horrible mistake in going back to him.

Eventually, I would learn that his "activities" had continued and even appeared to get significantly worse. I have no idea why Chris was behaving the way he was – I'm not a professional psychotherapist. I did not know if he was addicted to sex, or if he had some other behavioral pathology, or if he was simply repressing his obvious bisexuality. What was increasingly clear was that my husband was behaving in totally unacceptable and unsafe ways. These weren't just behaviors that violated our vows before God; these were behaviors that put me and our family at risk. My mind raced with questions and doubts. Was this adultery? Yes, it was. But it was also much, much worse than that.

It was a gradual progression. Chris went from being addicted to phone sex, to also being addicted to pornography. It then progressed to live video sex with strangers and eventually to meeting up with random men in parks. What was even more bothersome, was that Chris was rationalizing his behavior because he claimed he wasn't having penetrative sex with any of these men. Excluding penetrative sex (if I were to take him at his word) still provides a veritable smorgasbord of other sexual activity that certainly would constitute cheating, in my mind, or in the mind of any sane, rational person.

At the time, Chris worked in a furniture store. One day, he was alone in his office, and he started looking at gay porn. He didn't know, but his computer usage was monitored. His bosses watched, in real-time, while he looked up gay porn instead of doing his job. He was fired on the spot, and rightfully so. But now, this man's delusions and constant lies over his being gay had given rise to addictive behaviors that cost him his job. This was starting to impact me more than just emotionally and psychologically; now, there were real practical consequences.

I was livid and wound up kicking him out of the house. He moved down the street and in with a buddy of his. Soon, he'd get a job working in the oil fields and once again be able to provide for his children. But emotionally, I was a wreck at this point. The job meant that he'd go away for three to four weeks at a time and then come home for one week. In a bizarre way, I think his being gone so much was one of the main reasons the marriage lasted as long as it did. Being away for weeks at a time, allowed him to talk to men online, without being caught. His being away also gave me great peace and with the distance between us, I was able to see clearly how things really were. His absence also helped my anger to dissipate so that I could focus on what needed to be done – take care of my children. However, even though we continued with some distance between us, the marriage got increasingly more toxic. We started to hate each other; I certainly started to hate him. I was disgusted with him and his behavior, but more so, I was disgusted with myself for staying in a situation I knew to be very wrong.

I was, by no means, a perfect mom, but I was a good mom who loved her children and tried her best. In my defense, it is hard to be a perfect mom when your marriage is in shambles, and your husband is inflicting a particularly pernicious kind of abuse on your family. Children in such a situation are invariably affected, and I know that's the case for my kids. I also recognize that my children had to deal with a mom who was angry a lot of the time. I'm not sure they ever really understood why I was angry. I probably seemed angry at them some of the time, but they were never the reason I felt angry or frustrated, or trapped, or despondent. I felt all of these things because I was suffering silently.

In hindsight, I can think of any number of reasons why I chose to stay in the marriage: cultural and familial pressure, a desire to keep my family intact (unlike my parents, who divorced), and, almost certainly, a belief that I wasn't worthy of anything better. I never consciously felt as though I deserved such reprehensible treatment from Chris, but I did stay in the relationship far longer than I should have. We can remain blind to a great many things, not the least of which is infidelity. But I knew something was very wrong with my marriage, and it was having a negative impact on every facet of my life.

In terms of how dark things had become, I can remember in my desperation, praying to God for him to kill me so that I could escape my marriage. That should give you some insight into the degree to which I felt trapped, and, ultimately, out of any other options. Divorce simply wasn't yet a possibility. When I look back, I feel great empathy for myself in the throes of those emotions. At the time, death was literally preferable and a more realistic option to escape the marriage than feeling like a failure and walking away. This would all change; however, when I made a discovery that would eventually be my breaking point.

It was Easter and Chris had come home from the oil rigs to spend the week with his family. He was acting strange and distant and this made me feel uneasy. I had a sneaking suspicion that something just wasn't right. I saw his cell phone sitting on the table and thought to myself "here's an opportunity to see what's really going on." I opened his phone and within the internet history, I found an advertisement stating "Bisexual, married guy looking for fun." Along with the post was a photo of my husband's junk! My husband had uploaded an advertisement with a graphic photo of his penis in search of sexual encounters. The post had garnered a lot of responses and the conversations were quite explicit and disgusting. In the moments following this discovery, I then realized that my husband of fourteen years was trolling the internet for sex. This was another level of dangerous behavior that almost defies any sort of reasonable explanation – at least for a purportedly heterosexual married man. To say that I was mad would be a considerable understatement. I was disgusted and incensed. My husband was putting me and my children's welfare at risk. I knew instantly that my marriage was over. This was my last straw – he had gone too far.

The worst part is that it didn't end there. When I confronted Chris with the ad, he admitted that he was meeting random men in parks. He insisted that he hadn't had penetrative sex with any of these men, but how on earth could I trust a man who consistently lied to me and was disloyal? Even if he wasn't having full-blown sex with strangers, is giving or receiving hand jobs and blow jobs any less damaging? Of course, it isn't! It's outright cheating. It's infidelity. And it's also high-risk behavior that undoubtedly put Chris, me, and our children at risk. And for what means? Why would he put me and our children at such risk? Unfortunately, the answer is depressingly straightforward: to satisfy his desire for sex with men.

We had so many fights. Some were obviously aimed at both of us coming to terms with what was going on; most, however, were not. We had spiraled downwards in a toxic back-and-forth where we said horrible, hateful things. No matter what I tried, it wasn't working. In my heart of hearts, I knew that this was wrong. I didn't want to feel like I was breaking a vow to God, but I didn't think God would want me to stay in a marriage with a man who had no honor and who acted with cruelty and insensitivity towards his family. So, after all the effort and all of the willingness to look the other way, I just couldn't any longer. And I left.

All told, the marriage lasted 14 years. Considering that I discovered his infidelity, sex addictions, and bisexuality years prior, you can only imagine how difficult most of those years were for me. Still, I take responsibility for my staying in the marriage as long as I did. Leaving was absolutely the right thing to do. Once I confirmed that he was meeting strangers in parks, I ensured things were over between Chris and me by deliberately rekindling things with Paul. I had sex with Paul and then immediately told Chris what had happened. I wasn't going to allow him to degrade me any further, and I knew that my having been intimate with Paul would end things between Chris and I for good. Looking back, I wish I had the maturity and self-confidence to call him on his deception and just kick him out. But I didn't. I can't be too hard on myself - I got out of the marriage the best and quickest way I could at the time.

As you might expect, Chris did everything he could to frame things to my children and to his family so that I'd look like the bad guy. For me, taking the fall and admitting my affair with Paul, was easier than sharing with our children that their dad had a sex addiction spanning the entire duration of our marriage. While a select few close to me know some of these details, this is the first time that I am able to vulnerably share my truth. I had received, and continue to receive, horrible judgment from people who purported to be Christian simply for my refusal to stay in such a toxic situation. My truth is that my marriage didn't end because I was unfaithful, or because I was a bad person, or because I disregarded my vows. Sadly, my marriage ended because it didn't stand a chance from the beginning. The very foundation of my marriage was based on a lie, and it was only a matter of time before the marriage would crumble.

In the years since, he explained to our children that the marriage ended because of "their mother's multiple affairs." The way he has justified this in his own mind would be hilarious if it weren't also maddening and tragic. He considered my being with Paul during a break in year three of our marriage to be infidelity on my part because he and I were still technically married. Never mind the fact that I was only with Paul because I left Christopher after finding out about his phone sex addiction. I wasn't sneaking around or having an affair; I was trying to move on with a partner who actually wanted me. Then, when I left in year fourteen and had rekindled things with Paul, Chris considered that as affair number two. Again, this is despite the fact that he was meeting men in the park for sexual rendezvous. Still, we weren't yet divorced, so in his mind, he felt much better to paint this as my being unfaithful.

So, to set the record straight, especially for the sake of my children: I never had multiple affairs. My ex-husband certainly did, however. That is if you consider one-off sexual encounters with strangers to be affairs. And I'd say that's a fair characterization, all things considered. I am sharing this deeply sensitive and personal information because to this day, the relationship with my children is somewhat strained and distant and my hope is that this truth will help my children to understand the reasoning for their parents' separation and to come to terms with some of the decisions that were made. My hope is that any of the vicious lies and stories that have been told will be illuminated with truth and bare honesty so that together, our family can start to heal.

Christopher and I have now been divorced for over ten years. Ironically, Chris maintains a close relationship with my father, the man who refuses to acknowledge the existence of his biological children. On the one hand, I feel deep sadness that my father no longer has a relationship with me. And on the other hand, I feel anger and bewilderment that my father has continued to have a relationship with the man that cheated on, lied, and abused his daughter. I wish I were making this up! Sadly, I'm not, as my father and ex-husband talk regularly and are quite close.

In hindsight, even though I never really committed adultery, I can still take my share of responsibility for the marriage failing. I found myself playing the role of the martyr, which gave me something. It provided me with some kind of benefit. Otherwise, I wouldn't have stayed as long as I did. I can blame Christopher for his behavior, but at the end of the day, he didn't force me to stay in the marriage. I chose to stay in the marriage. And even though I was influenced by a variety of factors potentially outside of my control, the decision was still mine.

Over the years, I've developed a better understanding of how trauma affects development, and I've come to understand that exposure to trauma as a child likely contributed to my being codependent. My codependency is a major factor in my staying in the marriage. That isn't an excuse; my choices were and are my own. But it helps to explain why I made some of the decisions that I made and why, with the benefit of introspection, growth, and recovery, I'd make very different decisions today. This is what accountability is about. Ultimately, I chose to stay in a toxic marriage far longer than I should have. My codependent tendencies aren't an excuse; they're part of a much broader and more complicated explanation. I wouldn't make the mistake of staying in a toxic relationship today, but I didn't know then what I know now, and I wasn't equipped with the skills that I have now. I don't beat myself up over it, but I also don't pretend that I have no responsibility in the situation going on far longer than it should have.

So now, I was a single mom. I certainly didn't envision that I'd be here at this stage in my life, but I wasn't going to wilt under the challenge. I had children to take care of. And I had a life to rebuild. In the immediate aftermath of the divorce, Chris never missed an opportunity to show that I had made the right move. When we'd talk, he'd be so undermining and cruel. I'd talk about my plans to get a sales job to support myself and the kids, and he'd demean me at every turn. I can still hear his voice in my head, saying, "You can't get a sales job. You'll never make it in sales." Well, guess what? His disbelief in me only made me work harder. I was right to leave. As difficult as it's been, I've never regretted my decision to leave.

Sadly, I also remember a phone call that I got from my father in the immediate wake of my announcing to friends and family that the marriage was over. At first, I thought my dad was calling to check up on me. Your daughter's marriage falling apart due to her husband's constant infidelity is probably the kind of thing that warrants a check-in from most supportive, caring fathers. But that wasn't what this call was about. My father was urging me to stay in the marriage. He said,

"Chrystal, do you think that this is something that you could over-look?" I remember being part stunned and part disgusted. "What did you just say?" I asked. He changed his tone slightly. "I just mean, if you get divorced, one of your kids – at least one of your kids – will be fucked up." I hung up on him. I couldn't help but make the con-nection between himself, his own divorce from my mother, and the challenges my brother endured from the breakup of our parents. From one perspective, I guess he was speaking out of genuine concern for the children and his desire to see us avoid the same mistakes that he made. But he didn't really have a lot of credibility. I mean, asking your daugh-ter to stay in an abusive marriage was beyond comprehension to me. I was not about to take marriage advice from a man who had bailed at the first sign of trouble in his own marriage.

When someone starts their personal journey of self-discovery and healing, it becomes more apparent the generational trauma inflicted upon us. Childhood trauma comes in many forms, and as someone affected by childhood trauma, until you recognize the patterns and develop an understanding of where it originated from and make peace with it, those kinds of words and messages can be incredibly hurtful. It's not until we work through the painful words and actions and un-derstand where they are coming from (most likely from someone who has also experienced trauma), that we are then able to release the hold they have on us.

Five: Making Our Way

Life as a single mom wasn't easy, but it was much easier than living a lie and being trapped in a marriage where I felt I was losing my soul. Given my circumstances, I was incredibly happy that the marriage was over, at least after I let go of a lot of the guilt I was carrying about how it transpired and how it ended. I wanted a better outcome for my children, I tried everything to achieve just that. In the end, however, Chris' own addictions got the best of him and led him down a very dark path. I knew, deep down, that there was nothing that I could do to change that. It certainly hadn't been for a lack of trying. This was his path and only he would be able to reconcile how his behaviors affected our relationship.

With separation, however, I was able to reflect more on just how abusive the marriage had been and the extent of the suffering I endured during those dark years. One of the things that has stuck with me, and I continue to reflect upon, was how my childhood abuse was used against me as a tool to shame and control me. Chris was one of the few people in my adult life who saw firsthand some of the abuse I received at the hands of my mother. But instead of being supportive, loving, and protective, he actually used it to his advantage.

Because my mother had suffered from mental illness and had intermittent outbursts, there were times when, when Chris and I would fight, he would taunt me and call me by my mother's name. I can still hear his mocking, condescending voice, saying, "Is that right, Joanna?" It left me feeling not good enough, ridiculed, and belittled. His sarcasm was subtle, yet the message was clear. I was on the receiving end of narcissistic abuse and started to feel less than, insufficient and unworthy to be with him, let alone make it on my own. Because our marriage had become so unstable and toxic, we were fighting more and more often. And with the increase of daily disputes, came an increase in verbal attacks. I was feeling increasingly trapped, and his hurtful words were having a profound effect on me. I would later learn through my work in recovery that this kind of toxic cycle can cause brain damage in the victim. The persistent sense of feeling inadequate, anxious and in fear of one's own safety can keep cortisol levels unnaturally high, negatively impacting the brain. Repeated emotional "injuries" can also shrink the hippocampus (the area of the brain responsible for learning and memory) while enlarging the amygdala (the area that houses "primitive" emotions, including shame, guilt, grief, and fear.) With hindsight, that makes a lot of sense.

When I was experiencing these emotions, I was left feeling confused and uncertain about my own part in the breakdown of the relationship. How did I get here? With so much confusion and bouts of self-doubt, it took me quite a while to come to a place of clarity so that I was able to reflect on how harmful and toxic the relationship had been, especially toward the end. What's more, while this kind of reflection is incredibly difficult because it invariably involves exposing yourself to painful thoughts and memories, it is necessary for healing. Part of this healing process is courageously facing the hurtful acts committed and coming to terms with being an active part in the chaos.

Recognizing the red flags in any future relationship, romantic or otherwise, is a huge step in the process of healing and moving on.

As bad as my relationship with Christopher was, I do not regret it because I was blessed with four beautiful children. That's another important reason why I chose to work on forgiveness. Chris is the father of my children, and my children are my heart – they are part of both of us. In fairness, he was not a bad father; however, I struggle to say the same about his ability to be a good husband. In the years since our marriage ended, he has strived to be a good dad and my worries about him caring for my kids have subsided. Despite the painful memories of our marriage, I am now able to see the wonderful qualities that attracted me to Chris, reflected in our children. I feel proud that I have the maturity and capacity, especially in recovery, to appreciate all the positives of our relationship, despite it having failed.

It was 2014 when Chris and I separated. It then became paramount that my focus be on creating the best life possible for my children and myself. Finally free, and much to my own surprise, Paul re-entered my life. We rekindled our relationship, and in so many ways, things were just as they were before. Paul was wonderful. I felt alive and rejuvenated, as though I was reborn with a renewed thirst for life. I felt an immense sense of satisfaction to once again feel wanted by a man, to be an object of desire. I fell in love with Paul; we had a wonderful time together - being with him was easy. Even the second time around, there was nothing but love and acceptance; it was wonderful and very satisfying. Our relationship was a positive, healthy expression of love - quite the opposite of my experiences with Chris. Being with Paul was wonderful, but we eventually came to terms with the fact that we were very different people, and on very different paths in life.

As an extrovert, I think extroverts match up well with their opposites - introverts. In my experience, two extroverts together cause both people to constantly fight for attention. No one is happy to receive or let their partner express themselves without also wanting to be an active participant. The result is that the two extroverts wind up dissatisfied because they never have a proper audience. This was my experience with Chris, and it proved to be true, in our relationship.

Paul was absolutely an introvert, which meant that we matched up well. But eventually, I came to realize that he was quite reserved. He wanted to live a solitary life close to nature, and I was a mom with four kids! While we loved each other, it wasn't enough to overcome our significant differences. Still, we had wonderful times together, and I am grateful for having him in my life, especially during some of the most difficult times of my life. Not only did we share beautiful times, but ultimately, he helped me to get out of my marriage. His mere presence and contrast to Chris as a whole, showed me that things *can be* different, and that there *were* better, more complementary people out there *for me*. So, even though things didn't work out with us, he was a profoundly positive presence in my life. But now, it was just me and my kids, and I was determined to not just succeed, but to be the kind of role model that my children would be proud of.

Life as a single mom was bumpy at first, but quickly, I developed a real swing of things thanks to my incredible support system, which certainly includes my eldest children. Away from Chris, I was able to let go of so much of the anger and toxicity that had become so familiar in my life over the prior years. I began to realize how much healthier things were outside of the relationship, and most of my anger dissipated. Even today, while I continue to struggle with memories of the past, I am able to focus on my own journey, healing, and my personal growth. Today, I continue to work on letting go of the past, my perceived failures and flaws, and all the negative emotions that come with.

It took a few years to get into the swing of things, but things were shaping up to be quite the journey. Now in a new sales role, my professional life was starting to flourish. I was finally starting to be able to use professional talents entirely for my own benefit. My knack for public speaking and sales had always been a great benefit during my marriage to Chris, as we had had a highly successful business that had provided us with exceptional income and the ability to provide for our children. In retrospect, however, I was using a lot of my talents and gifts to facilitate the success we had. Now, on my own, I was able to put forth my talents for the benefit of myself and my children.

I threw myself into my work and was also making new friends and acquaintances. It was liberating, but it was also an extremely challenging time. My now ex-husband had left me with a $47,000 loan that was in his name and he was $50,000 in arrears for extra expenses - childcare costs, schooling, sports, and alimony, despite the court rulings for him to pay. I found myself sinking deeper and deeper into debt. My determination to prove to those who doubted me that I could and would succeed merely wasn't enough. I had found out about a "gifting circle" and thought it would be a wonderful way to create the security for my family that we needed. What a terrible irony that would soon come to be. But for now, my new life was taking on a whole new meaning and purpose. Unfortunately, I would soon be arrested, and everything would change.

Six: A Life Changed

In the days and weeks after my arrest, I felt as though I was in a daze. Would the police and Crown prosecutors realize that this was all a big mistake? Would this drag on for some time? I was filled with uncertainty and doubt, consumed by overwhelming thoughts and memories of my arrest, which took up residence in my mind, never leaving me to rest. This anxiety would serve as an important catalyst, not only in my addictions, but also in terms of changes to my personal relationships.

The criminal justice process in Canada has a limited amount of time to bring a case to trial. It starts from the time of arrest - the prosecutor must act upon the charges so as not to bottleneck the system for an indefinite period of time. The goal is to have cases move through the legal system with a certain amount of expeditiousness in accordance with general principles for justice. Therefore, if one is charged, they must be brought to trial within eighteen months. If they are not brought to trial, the case will be dismissed. Initially, I was hopeful that my charges would be dismissed very quickly; after all, I believed that my charges were unjust.

The case file is first reviewed by a Crown attorney. In my case, because I had been so open and forthright with the police, I was certain that everyone would have to agree that this was all a big mistake. It's hard not to laugh as I look back on writing this, especially with what I now know. But, when you're not versed in the criminal justice system, it's hard to imagine just how broken the system actually is, and it's inconceivable how vindictive and spiteful some of the people involved can be. To many, the system is a wicked game.

My lawyer recognized my optimism, and he provided some very wise, practical insight: he explained that it was not uncommon for Crown attorneys to drag out the process as long as possible. They very well could drop the charges, but if that happened, it likely wouldn't happen until right before the deadline for bringing the case to court, which happened to be the eighteen month deadline. I was so confused. It felt so spiteful and cruel to do things this way. If the charge was wrongful, heck, even bogus, then why would they want to prolong my suffering, waste taxpayer dollars, and jam up the system? The best answer I've since come up with is, quite simply, that they could.

There were other arrests in the Gifting Circle community. Other people – mostly women, just like myself, were arrested on this bogus charge, likely as part of the police's plan to discourage others from participating in the practice despite its clear legality. It seemed obvious that instead of doing meaningful investigative work, the police, for some reason or another, set their sights on preventing us from engaging in what was an entirely legal practice. I can only speculate on why that was. Perhaps it was because monetary gifts under a certain amount weren't taxable in Canada. Perhaps it was out of genuine concern that this was an illegal lottery due to investigative malpractice and general incompetence. Or, perhaps, this was rooted in the plain old-fashioned vehement envy and resentment of seeing a group of people enjoying themselves and getting ahead.

Initially, no one outside my personal circle would know about the arrest. However, the authorities made certain that this would change, once again, catching me off guard with further tactics to shame me and prolong the case. When it was clear the illegal lottery cases weren't proceeding as he liked, the lead investigator, Callahan, became determined to channel his frustration by leaking my name to the newspapers and local media, along with all the details of my case. I was paralyzed with humiliation. When I found out about what Callahan had done, I immediately contacted my lawyer. He explained to me that cops play this kind of "humiliation and shame game" but mostly with hardened criminals when the investigators felt that they were escaping justice. To my lawyer, this direct and purposeful attack seemed incredibly petty and needless. However, there was little recourse. Hell, I live in a country where cops kill innocent people and face few, if any, legal, social, professional, or other repercussions.

It's hard even to articulate the consequences to my personal and professional life that arose from this smear against me by the police. I was fired from a job I loved. My father stopped speaking to me. I had to deal with the embarrassment of friends and family possibly reading articles about how I was supposedly engaged in fraudulent activity. Meanwhile, money laundering in Vancouver was off the charts, and organized crime was running amuck. Yet, the police seemed to only be focused on what they considered a threat to society: me. It appeared that gifting circles represented such a tremendous risk to society and the social order in general that they (gifting circles) had to be stopped. Sarcasm intended.

In the aftermath of my arrest, I carried a lot of bitterness for the process. It was hard not to feel unjustly maligned and that it was a grotesque perversion of justice that public funds were being spent on investigating and arresting me when there was (and still is, mind you) considerable serious crime occurring in our communities - crime with serious social repercussions. Crime such as drug and human trafficking, money laundering through government-owned casinos to the tune of billions of dollars which is then used to facilitate other crime, both violent and non-violent, that exponentially creates serious costs to the system. Contrast this to a grassroots group made up of law-abiding moms and dads looking to give each other money, no strings attached. In my opinion, it was an abhorrent misuse of public funds.

Still, it happened. So, I had to work hard to frame things in a positive light and try to learn from my experiences. But in the immediate aftermath, I faced some extremely dark times. To cope, I turned to alcohol and drugs. Being directly shamed by society in the form of an arrest or public indictment posted in the press, much like I was subjected to, contributed to my existing feelings of shame. I had no idea that the unhealed shame and abandonment I had felt as a child would resurface and find its way back into my adult life. My turning to alcohol and drugs to cope only amplified this shame. In the throes of addiction, I often pondered the many twists and turns of my life, often waking up and thinking *"How the fuck did I get here? I'm not supposed to be here."* This shame often oscillated with anger and self-loathing and made me feel even worse, which only increased my appetite for more booze and cocaine. It was a never-ending vicious cycle, and I had become trapped.

My road to addiction was a slow burn – it didn't happen overnight. Things started very slowly and relatively innocently. I remember staring at that bottle of red wine the night of my arrest and thinking, *I need a drink.* I had never really felt like I needed a drink before, but I certainly did that night. In my mind, that's when the problem started. It all seemed relatively innocent at first. To understand how things got so bad, you need to understand the sequence of events as they unfolded.

At the time of my arrest, I had a great job that I loved in HVAC. Speaking frankly, I'm a bit of a geek – I loved HVAC which is typically a male-dominated field. I really enjoyed working to help others get the help that they needed in an industry I found fascinating. There was always something to learn, some new technology to become aware of, or some other development to stay on top of as part of providing the best possible customer service and support experience. My role was in sales. I went to customers' homes to inspect and determine their HVAC needs, then provided them with solutions based on their budget. I have always had a natural ability to form relationships where trust is developed quickly, and this allowed me to operate in a role where I was able to make good use of my interpersonal skills. I was well-received as the only female salesperson in the company. The role was great for building relationships, and I was very successful at it. The job wasn't just enjoyable; I made a great living and I was a high achiever for the company.

The police were six months into the investigation and were lacking support for the charges against me to bring me to trial. Because of their lack of evidence, and under pressure from the Crown, the law enforcement team working on my case leaked case details to the newspapers and television news outlets, pleading for any information to come forward. After several months, no one came forward. There was no information to support their charges against me - because there was no crime. It was eighteen months less one week that I was exonerated and released of any charges. In a moment of triumph, mixed with a grandiose arrogance, my criminal defense lawyer victoriously stated that he had just represented the first person in Canadian history to be charged – and exonerated – with running an illegal lottery. It had appeared that the authorities and the Crown wanted to use my case to set a country-wide precedent for illegal lotteries. I had been set up to be their pawn. I could not believe what I was hearing. I had been played from both sides. Illegal lottery charges had never existed in the history of Canadian law, and I was the first person to ever have been charged. Unsuccessfully, I might add.

It appeared that the company I was working for had become aware of a newspaper article relating to my charges. This was now seen as a problem by an employer who suddenly felt that I posed some kind of reputational risk. So, once becoming aware of my charges, I was immediately fired. In Canada, a company can terminate your employment with or without cause. If the company fires you without cause, they must provide you with severance. So, because I was let go without cause, I then hired a lawyer to sue my previous employer for an appropriate severance based on my achievements. Within a few weeks, I had received a settlement which just so happened to be the exact amount that I owed my criminal defense lawyer. While I was relieved that my legal bills were finally dealt with, I was then faced with the stark reality that I was now unemployed. This was yet another defining moment in my life – the moment in which I could feel every cell of my body start to boil with rage.

Seven: Love Lock Down

To understand the next stage of my journey is to understand how things ultimately went from bad to worse. At the end of August 2019, I met Dave. Dave was an outgoing, good-looking, magnetic man who drew all kinds of positive attention from just about anyone you could imagine. When I met Dave, my life was very much in flux; the immediate aftermath of the arrest was fading, but my life had still undergone considerable disruption, to put it mildly. I felt a huge weight lifted from my shoulders that the charges had been dropped, but it was hard to ignore the fact that I had been publicly humiliated, my reputation smeared, and I had been fired from the job I loved. To say that I had been through a lot was an understatement. I was ready for happiness.

Things moved quickly between Dave and I. By December of 2019, we were living together. I was unemployed (having lost my job due to the negative press release), I had emptied my savings to pay for legal fees and I was not receiving the court-ordered financial support from my ex-husband. All this led to me having an emotional breakdown. My inability to support myself and my children was one of the leading factors in my decision to move in with Dave and we started to build a life together. Dave asked me to marry him and on St. Patrick's Day of 2020, we married. Coincidentally, our wedding day was also the day that COVID lockdowns began across most of the world. The wedding day itself was beautiful. Our ceremony was outside, in a beautiful park setting, and it was an unusually gorgeous day for the month of March. It was a small wedding, with friends and loved ones. Looking back, I can clearly remember a feeling of happiness and contentment because everything seemed to be just perfect. This wedding, in many ways, was my do-over. I was ready for my happily-ever-after story, and at the time, I genuinely thought it was going to be with Dave.

In a relatively short amount of time, however, my new life with Dave would be fractured by a series of factors outside of our control. That April, Dave was laid off from his job in the transport division of the film and television industry. He regularly interacted with stars and big names in the movie industry, and he had a prominent business in film and television production. With COVID, however, most production had ground to a halt, which meant mass layoffs across many of the creative and support industries. At the time, I still wasn't working because I had been let go from my job a few months prior.

It was a time of transition. By this time, I had spent six years as a single mom; however, in reality, it was more like 17 years, having had an absent husband. I was so used to operating in the mindset of having to do things on my own, always having practical concerns about raising my children at the forefront of my mind. Now, I found myself in a situation where I was the every-other-week parent. I suddenly had more free time and I could explore a much greater range of opportunities. On the one hand, I missed my children dearly, yet at the same time, I wanted to embrace these new potential opportunities in the hopes of making a better life for them and for me. One such opportunity came that summer in the form of an Occupational First Aid Level 3 (OFA-3) course. I had spent enough time that summer lounging by the pool and now had a chance to improve my skills and took advantage of it. This opportunity would later become my career.

As fate would have it, I found myself browsing the employment ads, and one day I saw an ad that was for the lead sales rep for an HVAC supply company. This was – obviously – the kind of thing that was right up my alley. I had been in sales since I was twenty years old, and I loved HVAC. So, I applied, and of the twelve applicants, eleven of whom were men, I got the job. To say that I was incredibly proud and happy would be a significant understatement. What's more, they gave me ambitious targets to hit, so I had a real challenge ahead of me. As I recall, the initial goal was for me to take sales from 2.5M to 4M annually. This is a substantial increase, especially over a one-year time period. Still, I hit their goal two months early. So, within ten months' time, I had increased their sales by sixty percent. At one point, one of the senior managers jokingly said, "Ya know, Chrystal, you don't have to grow the business so fast!" However, working in HVAC also came with some challenges. It meant working in an old-school men's club type of environment. They can often struggle to deal with working alongside women because it breaks their mental models of what women are capable of and where they think women *should be* in the workplace. I was able to "crack the code" so to speak, and everyone loved working with me. I devoted all my spare time studying to master the industry, learning new technology and enhancing my skills. I wanted to be the best at my role as I could possibly be –and I was doing very well.

All of this played out against the backdrop of the complete and utter insanity of COVID lockdowns, made-up mandates, and public shaming of anyone who dared question the orthodoxy of the government and pharmaceutical companies. Personally, I wasn't comfortable with the degree to which this was being pushed on people. I thought people, at a very basic and fundamental level, should be given complete rights of bodily autonomy. I wasn't interested in being some vocal opponent to the vax, I believed people should be able to decide for themselves. So I exercised my right not to get the vaccine. I had seen the data that was available at that time, and, as a healthy person without any underlying medical conditions, I was comfortable with my body's own capacity to fight something like a coronavirus which had a 99.7% survival rate.

It was around October, and I had been in my sales role for a little over a year. The trade show season was coming up, and there was one particular trade show facility in Vancouver that mandated that the vendors had to be vaccinated. Immediately, I knew that this was going to be an issue. I went to my higher-ups and explained that I wouldn't be able to work that show. With that, it became clear that I was one of the few people in the company who hadn't been vaccinated. It was then that certain subtle and not-so-subtle pressures were applied to me. I was requested to attend a meeting with my bosses where I was asked "Chrystal, how do you think you're going to do your job?" I politely responded, *"Exactly, how I have been - with a 60% increase over last year's sales."*

At that moment, I knew what was coming. In hindsight, it's hard not to see through the subtlety of the question as being incredibly disingenuous. I calmly explained that the overwhelming majority of my role took place over the phone, and in cases where vaccination was required – like for this particular trade show – it was possible that one of the many other representatives could attend in my place. Realistically, it seemed like a non-issue. The only way that this would be a dire problem was if my bosses wanted to make it one. I would quickly find out that, yes, they absolutely wanted to make this a very big problem and ultimately, I was fired. After I was fired, I remember that oh-so-familiar feeling of rage, mixed with a sense of pride that I had stood by my principles and sound beliefs, no matter what the outcome.

Shortly after losing my job, I had started working with my husband in the movie industry, as a transport driver. That meant that my husband had also become my boss, and our lives quickly became entangled. It was an environment where we worked hard but played even harder. At work, I became aware of the double life my husband had been living – a life of deception and a penchant for admiration from other women that he worked with. On our days off, we plummeted into 24-hour cocaine and alcohol binges. Our life together spiraled out of control and became increasingly toxic and unhealthy. When the drugs ran out, it was as if we resented each other. It felt insidious, dark, and oppressive, filling us with feelings of disgust and repulsion for one another. It happened quickly and unsuspectingly, and I soon found myself doing cocaine on my own, hiding it from everyone in my life. It was all I knew how to deal with my increasing depression and feelings of hurt, rage, loathing and fear for my life. Ultimately, the cruelty and abuse I subjected myself to caused me to turn inward and my addictions took on a whole life of their own. My struggles started to get worse, and I felt myself being consumed.

It was the spring of 2022 when my brother died unexpectedly from an accidental overdose. He had struggled for years, covering up his own shame and trauma with the use of hard drugs. It shattered our family and caused us great pain, especially since I had now found myself in the same situation. I had confided in my sister how dire my life had become, so she invited me to Mexico to start my healing journey. My best friend, Karla, was paramount in encouraging me to take that first step. I was ready. I hopped on a plane and met my sister in Mexico, and it was there that my relationship with plant medicine began. Engaging with plant medicine in a safe and authentic way is a process that requires access to the right people, resources and a strong determination for change. My sister was already connected with a caring and respectable community of healers; she introduced me to the medicine community and expressed to me that I may find a similar benefit. I knew then and there that my life was about to change. In taking that first step, I was able to recognize how important my sister was in helping me to start the next chapter of my life and it showed me that indeed, I mattered. When I think back on this dark time in my life with the benefit of perspective, I can appreciate even more the extent to which my sister helped me to leave. I would not have had these opportunities were it not for her support and encouragement to start my own healing journey.

Shortly after returning from an incredible healing trip to Mexico, I found myself back at our house with my husband, Dave. It was July of 2022, and we had just started another movie project together called "*Buddy Games: Spring Awakening*" and I was tasked with being the personal driver of one of the main characters. I soon found myself in a situation where I had relapsed with my husband and things got bad very quickly. We were supposed to be in Harrison Hot Springs, a beautiful, picturesque lake town in the mountains of British Columbia, shooting the movie, but before we could leave the house, we had gotten into a very hostile and heated argument. It got out of hand so quickly; Dave exploded in a rage and had started ripping curtains off the walls and pulling things out of closets and throwing them all over the house. He tore out of the house, leaving to go to work, on his own, leaving me behind. I sat on my living room sofa in absolute shock and horror, shaking uncontrollably, unable to stop crying. *What had just happened?* I thought. In a desperate plea, tears streaming down my face, I cried out *"God, please help me. I can't do this anymore."* Within ten seconds (it may have been even less), my phone rang, and it was a friend, who lived and worked up north. She said *"Chrystal, I know this is a longshot and you're probably working right now, but I'm short a medic for a job I have to fill. Would you be available to start work on Monday?"* My heart leapt with a mixture of shock and gratitude. I said *"Book the plane ticket - I'll be there!"* In that moment, I knew that God had provided me with a way out. The OFA-3 course that I had taken months before had proven to be my saving grace. That was when my career as a medic started, and I have never looked back.

Eight: A Turning Point

A turning point can take many different forms and mean many different things for different people. Depending on our own journey, we may have one or multiple turning points. In my own journey, it's clear that I've had many; however, with hindsight, I can also pinpoint a particularly important shift in my perspective that helped to usher in change. At the same time, this wasn't the point at which recovery started; I still battled addictions to drugs and alcohol for some time. This, however, was the point at which things started to change in my mind. And, as anyone who's dealt with addiction will attest, the ideas you hold in your mind are of critical importance. If you believe negative things, your behavior will be impacted negatively. If you believe in positive things and believe that you're competent and capable of making necessary changes, your outcomes are much more likely to be positive as well.

I think my turning point really came toward the end of my relationship with Dave. Even though I had struggled with sobriety for some time after this, it was this time when things truly seemed the darkest. Later, in this book, I talk a little bit about rock-bottom and how a rock-bottom moment can serve as a catalyst for change. I don't think I had a single one of these moments; I probably had a few. One of these moments was when I tried to lick dropped cocaine up off the bathroom floor. It was this bizarre and humiliating moment that, I believe, led to an important re-connection with my brother. During a raw and emotional conversation with my sister, she shared with me that when our brother was alive, he had called her and explained that he had had a dream about me and was worried that I may be in trouble. Looking back, even though he wasn't consistently in my life at that time, I believe that he could see me in the throes of my addiction. Even though he wasn't there and didn't literally see me licking cocaine up off the floor, I do believe that he had that vision of me which reflected a relatively accurate picture of how I was struggling with my addiction.

Just as a side note to my dear readers – if you've ever wondered if you are addicted to cocaine, or any other substance for that matter, and you have found yourself licking it off a disgusting floor, please allow me to enlighten you of any further wonder. You are an addict. You are absolutely addicted to cocaine if you're licking it off a dirty floor. And that is the terrible thing about addiction; addiction can drive you to do appalling and shocking things that you'd never do otherwise. The shame that is perpetuated throughout this type of behavior is crushing. But please understand that if you can push through these bad feelings, you can better understand and ultimately neutralize the negative beliefs and feelings that drive your addictive behaviors. At this point in my journey, however, I was still struggling trying to neutralize my own beliefs and experiences. I was having moments of extreme darkness and deep despair, then having experiences of hope and salvation. I felt increasingly consumed by things outside of my control. Until which time, I started to realize that I couldn't do it on my own and I needed help. Help came in many forms.

~ ~ ~

One such dark moment was when I reached out to Dave's ex and the mother of his younger child. Christina had tried to warn me about Dave at the beginning of our relationship; she didn't want to see me go through what she had gone through several years earlier. At that time,

I had no interest in hearing anything negative about Dave and simply ignored her message. But my life had taken some very dark turns, and I suddenly found myself reaching out to this woman. Humbly, I admitted to her "You were right." She had every opportunity to turn her back on me, but she didn't. Instead, she reached out to me asking what she could do to help. Over time, Christina became my confidant; she was the one person I could speak to when I was wasted and in despair. She had spent hours upon hours with me on the phone, listening to me sob. She did not abandon me; she sat with me in some of my darkest moments. I never felt judged; I never felt shamed. I felt understood. I felt what I can only describe as unconditional love and support. To this day, we have remained great friends and I'm very grateful for her being in my life.

~~~

One night, I was visited by God (who I call Yahuah – I will talk about my specific religious beliefs a little later) when I was drunk and high out of my mind sitting on my kitchen floor. Lest you think I was just having a delusion or a psychotic break, I can assure you that this wasn't anything like that. The sense that you've been visited by God is absolutely one of the most profound experiences you can have because it is uniquely humbling. You know that no one will believe you if you attempt to describe what happened. You have an acute understanding of how anyone who hears the story will dismiss your confession as some sort of drunken fantasy. Yet, in many ways, this makes the experience all the more profound. The vision was deeply personal and powerful enough to get me to put a pause on my drug use. I resolved to cool it with the drugs and do an entire month of sobriety. Now that I was away from Dave, I could do just that.

It was most definitely one of the lowest moments of my drug addiction. One night, days into a red wine and cocaine binge, I found myself drunk and higher than a kite. I was sitting on my kitchen floor, sobbing uncontrollably. My cocaine use had innocently started out as fun and games but had gradually seeped into every corner of my mind, causing me mental anguish and turmoil. My thoughts had started to turn on me, the voices in my head jeering and taunting each other. I remember saying aloud, my voice filled with contempt, *"Hey Jesus, you said you'd never leave or forsake me. Where are you now, when I need you the most?"* I tried to pick myself up off the floor, sobbing and full of anger, when suddenly, I fell to my knees. I started to pray to God. I was in a stance of complete and utter surrender. I couldn't get up. I cried out *"Jesus, save me. I can't go on like this any longer."* In that moment, His glory filled the entire room. I felt a sovereign strength that provided me with the strength to stand up and suddenly, I felt as though I was on a stage, His bright lights shining down upon me. I became filled with His Word. As I stood on that stage, the words of the Bible poured out of me, and I was enveloped with his luminous glory. For three hours, I spoke scripture until I was completely sober, and the effects of the cocaine had completely worn off.

~~~

God had met me in my complete and total surrender. But that was just the beginning. I then had to become completely honest and vulnerable and confess my need for help to those closest to me. It was only in that moment of raw truth and ultimate surrender that I was able to admit and ask for the help I so needed. God had imparted a strength within me, and I then knew that I was able to overcome my addiction. He had waited until I had to come to a point of utter desperation and complete surrender to finally ask for His help. It was in my deepest, darkest moment that the following verse of the bible came to mind: Psalms 40:2 "He lifted me out of the slimy pit, out of the mud and mire; he set my feet on a rock and gave me a firm place to stand." It's in this verse that King David promised that once the Lord delivered him, that he would go back to help others. That day, standing on that stage, He gave me a glimpse of my future: that I would revisit the muck and the mire to help pull out the others, and ultimately set the captives free. To this day, with more than one year of sobriety, I stand in honor of my promise to Yahuah, my Savior.

.

Nine: The First Ceremony

It's important to understand that people turn to plant medicine for any number of different reasons. And, in many cases, I think it's fair to say there's both variance and overlap in terms of the reasons people choose to explore plant medicine. Some people may want to explore plant medicine as a means to heal trauma while simultaneously wanting to have a psychedelic experience, a bonding experience, or an adventure.

Regardless of your own reasons for being interested in plant medicine, it's important to know that it can take many forms and involve a vast range of different substances and activities. These can range from the relatively mild, which may provide psychedelic or introspective experiences, to the much more powerful ones, which are capable of providing profoundly dislocating experiences that can destroy one's ego or create significant psychological distress. There can also be physiological risks associated with plant medicine.

At this point, I should note that while I refer to my experiences as having been with plant medicine – and they were – I also had a number of experiences with frog medicine, specifically Kambo and Bufo (also called Bufo Alvarius or *sapito*). Like plant medicine, frog medicine has long-established traditions among Indigenous groups in

South America and Northern Mexico and the Southwest of the United States, respectively. Also, like plant medicine, these are powerful medicines that must be respected. There are a variety of risks associated with taking these medicines, and so working with experienced, reputable practitioners is key. Be mindful that there are a lot of charlatans and inexperienced people masquerading as facilitators in this field. So, there are risks associated with actually finding a reputable facilitator as well as taking these substances. For all of these reasons, a considerable breadth and depth of research into sacred plant and frog medicine is wise for anyone interested in wanting to learn or potentially undertake their own experience one day. Prior to my own personal experiences, I had spent a lot of time researching their effects to gain a deeper knowledge and understanding. I also sought out people who had used these medicines to help foster their own recovery from addiction.

Even still, I was really nervous. First, I was nervous because it was a very different drug than what I was used to. A psychedelic experience involves a loss of control that you don't get from cocaine, for example. Second, I knew that plant medicine had the potential to drive the participant to make powerful but often painful revelations and discoveries.

The plan was to start with a tobacco purge (a ceremonial cleansing of the physical, mental and energetic bodies) and then have two ayahuasca ceremonies back-to-back; however, my flight to Mexico was delayed, and I missed the tobacco ceremony the first night of the retreat. I'm sure my having missed the tobacco purge did affect how I experienced the ayahuasca ceremonies.

It was the first of two ayahuasca ceremonies and to begin, participants were offered a mix of tobacco and other plants called rapé, also called *hapeh*, and mapacho. I didn't partake on the first night because I was totally uncomfortable with the idea of putting something up my nose. You have to remember I'd been struggling with a cocaine addiction, and I'd been sober for only a few weeks. When it was time for ayahuasca to be served, each participant went to the altar, where the curandero was seated, and drank their cup of ayahuasca, a brew made of the ayahuasca vine and the Banisteriopsis caapi bush. With ayahuasca, participants typically experience a purging reaction – it will either come out of one end or the other or manifest in the form of sweating, chills, yawning, shaking, burping, crying, to name a few. In my case, the medicine hit me very quickly, and I began to vomit. I can't recall ever vomiting so much or so hard. It felt like a never-ending amount of crap that I was able to eject from my body. Just when I thought that the worst was over, I'd be struck by another wave.

Ayahuasca medicine is typically used in sacred spiritual ceremonies. Classified as an *entheogen*, it allows for the participant to access a higher state of consciousness. Being more sensitive, it allows for the purging of toxins and old emotions from trauma and addiction that become stored in the body. If you have never experienced it, it sounds more than a little bizarre to talk about vomiting and diarrhea as being a healing response to trauma or addiction, and many people would shy away from the thought of vomiting – especially in a group setting. But these are very normal and acceptable parts of the ceremonies, and ultimately, the release process, and are incredibly healing.

After I had finished purging, I remembered my body feeling physically exhausted. Even though I had been sober for the last few weeks before the retreat, my body was really suffering from the effects of my lifestyle. I had stopped exercising, I wasn't eating right, and my body was letting me know that everything that I had been doing came with consequences. I was completely exhausted and weak from the physical purge – I could barely move. I remember laying my head on the cement surface of the maloca (the temple in which ceremonies are held) and just staring into complete nothingness. Suddenly, my eyes fixed on a beetle. It was a scarab beetle, and he was a frantic ball of energy, so busy, working hurriedly with clear purpose and dedication. I remember looking at him and thinking to myself, *"What are you doing? Why are you such a busy little beetle?"* His busyness held my attention and eventually, he morphed into Pacman, hurriedly making his way through a maze. I couldn't, for the life of me, lift my head off the ground. I drifted off to sleep.

An ayahuasca ceremony can last anywhere from six to maybe twelve hours, depending on the strength of the brew. In the morning, once the medicine has worn off, there is a time of sharing and integration – an extremely important part of any sacred medicine ceremony. Integration allows you to share your experience and also hear the experiences of others, providing you with a greater understanding and insight into your own journey. At the end of the morning, when many people were getting ready to leave, I went to Fia, the curandera (healer) to hopefully gain more insight into the meaning of the beetle. She was placing beautiful, colorful tapestries on the ground that she had brought from Peru. That's when I saw a tapestry that was exactly what I had seen in my vision. *"Hey! It's the beetle!"* I exclaimed. The tapestry was made of a gorgeous red and purple pattern that looked just like the Pacman maze that I'd seen the night before. I shared with her everything that I had seen and how I thought this tapestry represented the busy little beetle. She smiled. *"Interesting."* She went on to explain that there were different ways of looking at the situation based on my personal life experiences. I listened intently, fascinated and captured by her every word. Seeing as the beetle is a symbol of rebirth, regeneration, health and protection, we concluded that that little beetle was rewiring my brain, creating new neural pathways and forming more positive and healthy connections in my brain!

My first experience with ayahuasca was beautiful and profound, all things considered. It also didn't hurt that we were in an incredibly beautiful environment out in the jungle of Quintana Roo, Mexico. The next day, I woke up to monkeys playing outside my hut.

That night, we would do our second ceremony. Having had such a positive experience my first night, I was game to partake in the rapé the second night. I had the bright idea that I should try to conquer my fears and just do it. For the uninitiated, rapé is a finely ground mixture of tobacco and other medicinal plants and herbs that is blown up the nostrils by the curandero/a with an instrument called a *Tepi*. It is widely used by indigenous tribes and is believed to cleanse the mind, body, and spirit, offering the recipient an ease of access to higher states of consciousness and it can also provide a calming effect by ceasing the brain chatter, depending on the different medicinal herbs used in the mixture (there is a wide range of mixtures available for any number of situation or medical issue). It also works to decalcify the pineal gland.

The curandera blows the rapé in each nostril, one at a time, starting with the left nostril, representing feminine energy, and then the right nostril, representing masculine energy.

Fia started with my left nostril, the feminine side, and I immediately felt incredibly sick and anxious. My heart was pounding, and I could barely catch my breath. She comforted me but then explained that she needed to do the second nostril – the right and masculine side. I gathered my composure and leaned in to receive the second blow. Fia raised the Tepi and inserted it into my right nostril and blew. It was nothing like I had ever experienced. The rapé entered my brain like a gunshot to my head. I was gone, flat out on the floor in the middle of the maloca convulsing, sweat pouring from every pore of my body. I couldn't move. I didn't realize it at the time, but my body was engaged in an extensive detoxification process. All the coke and garbage I had put into my body over the years was pouring out of me. I went in and out of consciousness, at one point having a vision of angels standing over me, waving fans over my body to cool me off and bring me back to consciousness. Once I did come to, Fia lovingly and gently explained that it wouldn't be a good idea to have ayahuasca that evening because of my strong reaction to the rapé. So that night, I flowed in and out of consciousness while listening to the healing sounds of the most beautiful medicine music I've ever heard.

Ten: Recovery From Addiction is Not Linear

Human beings like to simplify things. There's an evolutionary reason behind this; we have a need to recognize patterns. Being able to boil things down to their essence is helpful for understanding patterns. Unfortunately, however, our need to simplify things often leads to our great misunderstanding of them. In the case of addiction, and more specifically, recovery from addiction, someone not directly affected might think that recovery takes a particular form and that we can trace a somewhat predictable, replicable path. Unfortunately, things are much more (and frustratingly!) complicated than that.

Despite the fact that I was actively working on my recovery, I was still engaging in drug and alcohol abuse. I wasn't deliberately trying to split myself in two; I was focused on recovery, but I also hadn't completely gained the skills needed to meaningfully support my recovery and sobriety over time. In case that sounds like a cop-out, it isn't. If you're struggling with addiction, and especially if you've experienced relapses, you know that there can be a disconnect between what your rational mind wants and what your body can actually support. Beating yourself up about it isn't just unhelpful; it's totally counterproductive.

This goes back to Bradshaw's explanation of addiction rooted in trauma perpetuating a kind of all-encompassing shame that tells the person suffering from it that they are inherently bad, unworthy, and incapable. There's a cliche in popular culture related to addiction; you've probably heard it before. We sometimes tell addicts that they need to suffer a "rock-bottom" moment from which recovery is possible. The idea is that you experience what feels like your lowest moment due to your addictions and the ensuing havoc they've wreaked in your life. The realization that you are at your lowest serves as a catalyst for change, and recovery starts to be possible. I think everyone is different, but I do think that many of us do experience a "rock-bottom" moment, one that crystallizes with hindsight and serves as a reminder to us of just how bad things got.

In my case, I feel like there were a few rock-bottom moments. The realization that I was trapped in an abusive relationship with a man who terrified me was certainly one. But, looking back, I'd say there were others, too. Another rock-bottom moment I mentioned earlier was licking cocaine off a dirty floor. I don't know if it's possible to describe how awful it feels to be addicted to cocaine, not have any cocaine, and be too intoxicated or fucked up to do anything about it. However, I'm going to try to paint an honest and detailed visual to help you understand.

You know the feeling that creeps in on a Sunday evening as you start to think about all of the work you have to do during the week ahead? If you love your job and situation, this feeling may be fairly mild – heck, you might not even experience it at all. But I'm sure that most of us can relate to the feeling of dread, at least at some stage of our lives. Let's say that you don't like your job and perhaps you work with a toxic boss that has unreasonable expectations and micromanages you. You may be on the receiving end of negative feedback, leaving you feeling insecure, making your days at the office unbearable. Or you may be young, struggling to get by and therefore need to work multiple unsatisfying jobs. The week ahead feels like a chore. With the knowledge that your brief reprieve is over, a feeling of dread and anxiety starts to come over you.

Now, imagine multiplying that feeling by numerous times over. Add in symptoms of physical withdrawal. Now, add in the multitude of symptoms that come with alcohol abuse. I am entirely cognizant of the fact that I began to experience very brief (but very real) dissociative effects from my addictions. Depersonalization-derealization disorder works to affect how a person perceives reality. It isn't a form of psychosis; rather, it is a dissociative condition in which the person affected starts to feel unlike themselves or like the world around them isn't real or what it seems.

People in the throes of chemical addictions can experience depersonalization-derealization and other dissociative disorders. Indeed, many addicts descend further into psychological mayhem and actually do experience psychosis – a psychotic break with reality characterized by actual hallucinations and hearing voices. I never experienced psychosis, but I do remember briefly feeling dissociated and having moments where I kind of felt like I was living in an alternate reality. It was terrifying, and these moments signaled to me that I was on a razor's edge with my addictions and that I needed to keep working toward sobriety and, ultimately, recovery.

Still, I didn't have the skills or other resources I needed to stay sober. I felt terrible shame, which drove additional use. But I was desperate for healing, and it wouldn't be long before I'd get another incredible opportunity to engage with plant medicine, once again, thanks to my sister.

Eleven: The Second and Third Ceremonies

Given my ongoing struggles with addiction and the ensuing emotional, practical, and psychological problems that come with such issues, I jumped at the chance to give plant medicine another try. My first experience had been profound; still, I knew that it hadn't entirely had the effect that I wanted. I'm not saying I naively expected a sacred plant ceremony to immediately eliminate my addiction issues, but that was why I was pursuing this: for recovery.

I had the opportunity to take a trip to Peru, to work with Fia again. I knew that there would be a chance to partake in both tobacco and temazcal ceremonies. My experiences with ayahuasca were powerful but left me wanting more in terms of self-reflection, insight, and discovery. So, I hopped on a plane – by myself – on a two-week trip to Peru, where the prospect of learning and engaging with tobacco and temazcal ceremonies were intriguing.

Despite my previous experience with tobacco during my profound rapé ceremony in Mexico, I didn't really understand the depth of meaning and purpose of tobacco. I quickly learned that tobacco has incredible healing properties and is a powerful maestro (teacher or master). Tobacco, or Father Tobacco, causes a deep cleansing effect; it allows the clearing of physical toxins by way of "the purge," eliminating

101

toxic elements, thoughts, and feelings from the body. It is considered the 'king of the jungle' because it is the largest plant, and it tends to push out invasive species or other plants. It is worth noting that tobacco "tea" purges are effective not only for tobacco addiction, but also in general for any dependence involving misuse. Moreover, in a ritual context, vomiting also encompasses the purging of "toxic" thoughts and feelings as a result of that misuse. Tobacco purges restore proper circulation and health within the body, mind, and spirit.

I can remember sitting in a circle as part of the first tobacco ceremony. Fia, the curandera, had prepared a tobacco drink that we were all to consume. Even before I had a sip of that tea, I remember starting to weep. Overcome with emotion, with care and a sweetness in her voice, Fia assured me that this was normal and that I would be okay. After drinking the tea concoction, I remember a pure and genuine feeling of gratitude wash over me. I remember saying, *"Thank you for this. Thank you for my life."*

Suddenly my father's face flashed before my eyes. I had no sense or feeling of anger, resentment, or coldness; instead, I felt genuine gratitude.

I softly whispered, *"Thank you for giving me life,"* and I meant it.

And as I was overcome with this feeling of gratitude, I suddenly also felt waves of forgiveness wash over me. I wasn't angry at him any longer. I felt nothing but gratitude.

That ceremony gave me such a unique feeling of closure and peace with what had been, up to that point, an ugly and traumatic chapter of my life. The anger that I had felt because of the arrest and my father not talking to me, had finally washed away. I was left feeling immense gratitude for his giving me life and I had finally come to a place of understanding for my father's own traumas.

At the time of writing this, I still have had no contact with my father. While I experienced a great sense of forgiveness and understanding during my ceremony, I cannot condone some of his behaviours that have greatly affected me. I still hurt because of my father's choice to remain friendly with my ex-husband yet turn his back on me. I respect his choices, even if I don't understand them. I genuinely feel that if he wanted to have a relationship with me, I would be open to having one.

Ironically, as my relationship with my birth father disintegrated, my relationship with my Heavenly Father has since grown much stronger. Today, I feel the constant presence of my Heavenly Father, guiding me and helping me in my day-to-day life. I am grateful to Him, for connecting me to so many beautiful people, for connecting me to great jobs and opportunities, and for giving me the strength to recover from my addictions. In this sense, what my birth father couldn't do for me, my Heavenly Father has. I am truly grateful.

My third experience with sacred medicines was profoundly different than the first two. Not just because different substances were involved but because, this time, I experienced profound revelations especially relevant to my trauma and recovery. In my case, frog medicine, specifically Bufo Alvarius or *sapito*, was an important catalyst for spurring these revelations.

Frog medicine refers to ceremonial and ritualistic healing practices common among Indigenous groups, especially in places like South America (Kambo) and Sonora, Mexico (Bufo). Once again, my sister had introduced me to a Mexican lady and healer who used frog medicine with her clients, and I was extremely interested in trying it. She would serve as my guide to both Kambo and Bufo Alvarius.

Kambo is a healing ritual of South American origin that uses the venom of giant monkey frogs. It has been used by Indigenous groups all over South America for centuries, but in recent years, it has been growing in popularity among those interested in alternative healing practices. It is referred to as a venom; however, it is not poisonous to the human body, and in fact, the opposite is true. In the ceremony, the venom is applied onto a raw part of your skin prepared to receive the medicine. The relatively intense method of administration puts a lot of people off. Kambo has unique peptides that help to restore wellness in the body by resetting your nervous system and cleansing the liver; it has antiviral effects and helps with immune system modulation; it has antimicrobial properties, anti-inflammatory effects and aids with blood pressure regulation, setting the stage for your potential recovery.

This cleansing is both metaphorical and practical; by drinking copious amounts of water, the Kambo venom aids to flush the toxins out of your body by way of either vomiting or having an alternative gastrointestinal resolution, if you catch my drift (yes, I'm talking about diarrhea.)

Kambo is serious business and I would only advise someone who could access a reputable, experienced guide to partake. Moreover, the nature of Kambo is such that it doesn't yield a particularly psychedelic or even enjoyable experience. I only partook because I was with very experienced and knowledgeable guides, and I was desperate for healing.

Kambo stands in contrast to Bufo, which is a similar but different kind of frog medicine. Unlike Kambo, Bufo Alvarius is the excretion from the Colorado River Toad found mostly in the state of Sonora, Mexico and in some parts of the southern United States. The excretion is dried; this dried, powder-like substance is then heated in a crack pipe-looking device, which turns into a vapor and is then inhaled. At a molecular level, Bufo contains 5-MeO-DMT, an alkaloid with hallucinogenic effects. I've done Kambo once and Bufo twice. I've found both to be extremely powerful substances that – while not necessarily enjoyable - both were helpful in my journey toward recovery and healing.

Bufo is extremely strong, producing concentrated shifts in perception, often described as spiritual or mystical events. Most experiences range between 20 and 45 minutes and there is a complete and total loss of control. I will repeat myself again on this subject: if you're going to explore the value of these substances for your own healing, you must absolutely work with knowledgeable and experienced practitioners. Frog medicine, much like plant medicine, is extremely powerful. Make sure you don't just do it because it's available; do it properly, respectfully and with intention.

The healer I worked with was an expert who had a safe and supportive environment prepared for me to undertake my journey. We were outside, in nature, amongst a backdrop of trees and the sounds of a river trickling nearby. I smoked the dried substance from the pipe; the smoke had an acrid taste to it, but it wasn't revolting; it was odd. I wondered why it was so - palatable, for lack of a better word, but before long, my wondering stopped. I had totally dissociated from my immediate surroundings and I was traveling down a tunnel of bright light. I felt as if I was in the middle of space, on some kind of trip, but from here to… where?

I suddenly heard a voice ask, "What's one of your earliest memories?"

Before the voice had even finished asking the question, I couldn't start to speak the words fast enough. I knew exactly what it was; I'd thought about this memory a lot. It never really made a lot of sense to me as some parts were missing and others a blur. I never really understood its significance, but I knew exactly what it was.

I was suddenly transported back to my childhood. I was in my living room; my sister was there, my brother was there, and I was crying. There was a mustard-colored chair. I was crying. Did I say I was crying? I was crying.

I don't know why I was crying.

The voice, ignoring my stammering proclamations, asked me outright, "Why were you crying?"

Why was I crying?

I snapped back to the ceremony. I was sweating profusely, my mind racing in confusion. My mind started to drift.

Looking back, I wasn't capable of having a rational sequence of thoughts. I was experiencing more of a steady stream of consciousness that drifted from one place to the next. Some of my thoughts were fully formed, but in other cases, I'd have flashes of a vision in black and white.

In one vision, I was fixated on the mustard-colored chair from my living room growing up. Why was I crying? In another, I could see my mom hit my sister. Did that make me cry? In still another vision, I thought about my brother.

My next thought was about being in a physiotherapist's office. I've had neck problems for as long as I can remember. Years ago, when I was taking an annual physical with a new doctor, she said she found pronounced scar tissue at the base of my neck. She asked, very straightforwardly, "Have you ever broken your neck? There's a big lump here on your C1."

I was totally taken aback.

"No?" My facial expression clearly indicated that I needed some more information from the doctor.

"Oh, you just have a lot of scar tissue here, that's all." I wracked my brain to try to find a specific incident that would be the cause of such an injury.

"What could cause that?" I asked.

"You could have suffered a minor break when you were little. It happens sometimes. Do you experience a lot of neck pain?"

Suddenly, I was jolted from the doctor's office. I was seeing stars. Thousands of stars, and they seemed to be alive, twinkling at me.

I started to feel sick. I hoped that I wouldn't throw up, or worse, what if I – just as that thought finished in my head, I was gone again and back in my living room. I then heard the soft rustling of the leaves on the trees and the sweet sounds of birdsong in the distance. Now, a bell. Music. A sweet angelic voice……

It suddenly all made sense. It was like the medicine was speaking to me. Not literally speaking but communicating without words. Understanding washed over me, and I was back in my childhood living room. I could see the living room clearly; I could see my brother and sister. I could see the mustard-colored chair. And now, I could see my mother.

My mother was yelling frantically. She had a wooden spoon in one of her hands. The sight of her with a kitchen utensil stands out in my mind because she'd frequently hit us with a wooden spoon, and anything else that was in arm's reach.

First, I felt relief at the mystery being solved. I remembered the rest of the memory! It was as if the medicine prepared me, asked me if I was ready, and then, when I surrendered completely, the medicine showed me what had happened on that horrible day. As I felt myself floating, I felt a wave of bizarre emotions.

Relief gave way to fear and pain. Like I was watching a movie, I saw my mother grab me by my hair, my tiny body being lifted up from the carpet as I was tossed across the room. I crashed down onto the living room floor, sobbing hysterically. Now, I wasn't viewing it from an external perspective - I was now five years old. I looked up to see the mustard- colored chair, and I saw my sister and my brother both standing over me, horror written all over their faces.

I was suddenly jolted from the movie – or was it a memory? - and I returned to the ceremony. The medicine had just shown me that this nagging memory was of my mother throwing me across the room in a fit of rage. My neck had been broken. I suddenly understood.

One of the hallmarks of a Bufo trip is that you cannot control your mind – the medicine controls you. Your mind goes where it goes. So this wasn't some deliberate fantasy or my just seeing something I wanted to see. It was so incredibly painful and traumatic that I really didn't want to make that realization. But I wanted the truth and I'm convinced that more of the truth had been revealed to me.

It was – and is – an incredibly painful realization to make. But it was necessary for my healing and, ultimately, my recovery. Acknowledging the trauma that little Chrystal endured is so important because it helps me to have empathy for myself and to recognize that my internalized shame and addictive behaviors didn't just stem from my arrest or the bad things that happened to me with Chris or with Dave. My childhood was mired in trauma, and developing a real understanding of that – complete with memories I had tried to repress – could allow me the insights needed to continue my healing.

Memories are repressed as a means of psychological and emotional protection. When things are simply too painful, our mind blocks them out. We forget events, we forget details. Our mind protects us. So opening these wounds is painful but ultimately necessary for healing. This is one of the reasons I take sacred plants and other alternative medicines so seriously. You have to be prepared for them to reveal things, to expose things that will cause you great pain, even if such revelations are ultimately beneficial and healing.

I thought long and hard about this new revelation, including what it meant to my understanding of my youth, my mother, and my own tendencies as a mom. At first, I wasn't sure if I should confront my mother with the realization. On the one hand, we're told that communication about important issues is critical in your familial relationships. On the other hand, I knew my mother. I knew that from a practical perspective, she literally might not remember the incident in question. As I've explained, besides suffering from mental health issues, my mother has battled a serious substance abuse issue. She regularly took pills and after years of abuse, these kinds of behaviors, especially over the long term, are known to have a serious impact on memory. But on the other hand, she might very well remember the incident, and if she did, she'd almost certainly deny it. Narcissists do not do well with self-reflection and accountability, especially when you're asking them to admit that they did something terrible and take accountability.

This last experience with Bufo was deeply traumatizing, and I haven't had much interest in pursuing additional work with frog medicine. Speaking honestly, there is a part of me that is afraid of other visions that might be revealed. Coming to terms with that repressed memory has been extremely empowering, but it has come at a real cost in terms of the emotional work required to process what happened and to come to terms with it. There may come a time in the future when I think I'd like to further explore what frog medicine can show me and the insights I can gain. For now, I am grateful for the experiences I've had and am happy to leave it at that.

Twelve: Coming Home

Ironically, focusing on strengthening my relationship with my mother led to me making one of the most powerful human connections I've ever experienced. As I've noted, despite my history with my mom, we do maintain a loving relationship, for which I am grateful. We started to talk more, and she would go on about this one particular neighbor of hers, Alain. Honestly, I think she had a bit of a crush on him, even though she was old enough to be his mother. I also think there was a part of her that connected with him because he reminded her of her late son, my brother. She'd talk him up, and eventually, I thought to myself, I should probably meet this guy to see what all the fuss is about.

I'm dating myself here, but readers of a certain demographic will remember the 90's TV sitcom *Home Improvement*. For those unfamiliar with the show, it featured a neighbor character, Wilson, whose entire face you'd never see. The viewers could only see the top half of Wilson's head from across the main character's backyard fence. It was a running gag, keeping the audience in suspense of just who this person was. They'd throw up all kinds of implausible situations and happenings to keep the audience from ever seeing the bottom half of Wilson's face. I had comical flashbacks of watching an episode of *Home Improvement* the first few times I saw and conversed with Alain. Chatting back and forth across the balcony railing that separated my mom's and Alain's apartments, barely able to see his entire face, brought me back to the humor and silliness of the sitcom.

At first, we chatted about mundane, everyday things – like the weather, or ordinary day-to-day issues in life. He was very handsome, but he wasn't the type I had typically gone for in my past, so I didn't find myself instantly smitten. I knew from my mom that Alain was a recovering addict. At the time, I had no idea what he was addicted to, but I remember thinking, "He was probably addicted to opioids." Looking back, it wasn't anything specific that gave way to me thinking this – it's a very common addiction in today's society and sadly, it's something a lot of people struggle with.

Believe it or not, that belief caused me to look down on him - like my cocaine addiction was just way more acceptable than a lowly opioid addiction. Obviously, it was a very facetious and inaccurate thought, but I really did think that at the time. I think we do such mental gymnastics when comparing our addictions to others, so much so that we fight to come up with some ridiculous ideas and excuses about how things compare. Anything to make it seem like what we're doing isn't really as bad as it could be or as bad as what someone else is doing.

At the same time, I felt an instant connection with Alain. I wasn't sure what role he'd play, but I immediately knew that he would play an important role in my life. Right away, I could tell he was attracted to me, which put me off. You have to remember; I hadn't had the best experiences with committed relationships. It was natural for me to feel guarded and defensive in regards to any kind of potential romantic interest. In the end, however, I decided to give him my phone number.

At the time, I was working on remote work sites as a medic, which wound up being an incredibly positive thing for maintaining my sobriety. If there's no access to alcohol, you can't drink, no matter how much you might want to. So, I'd be on site for three weeks at a time, and I dove into reading, listening to podcasts, focusing on my self-improvement and personal development. I had gone through my second divorce, and part of me was genuinely disappointed and wondering how I ended up here. I had resolved to take responsibility and really consider the role that I had played in why these things had happened.

More and more opportunities arose where I was able to talk with Alain, and talk we did. He wound up being an incredible confidant. He had worked as a drug and alcohol counselor for 14 years after being a recovering addict. He wasn't just a great listener; he really understood a lot of the things I shared with him and he offered great insights that were truly helpful. We talked for hours – sometimes four, or five hours at a time.

Unfortunately, he had suffered a six-year relapse, but had been sober for the last 18 months prior to our meeting. My head was filled with so many conflicting ideas and concerns about Alain. We had an incredible connection, but I didn't know if I could rely on him to maintain his sobriety. Ultimately, we developed an intense bond, and when I'd travel to Vancouver to visit family, I'd stay with him. We were becoming incredibly close. We were becoming a couple. That, in and of itself, caused me shame, and I worried about other people finding out and being judgmental because of my past relationships that had ended so badly.

As soon as we gave into the obvious chemistry between us, I fell hard and fast. He treated me with such care and affection. It was a very positive, affirming experience, but short-lived. It wasn't long after we came together romantically that I suffered a relapse. The road to recovery isn't a straight arrow from A to B. That's just how it is. I knew enough by that point that beating myself up over it or pretending it didn't happen would only make things worse.

When I confided in Alain, he did not handle it well. And, honestly, I completely understood. He was worried about maintaining his own sobriety, and rightfully so. The dynamic of our relationship changed after that, even though we still maintained a loving friendship. He said straight up that he couldn't be with me if I was going to relapse, and I was knowledgeable enough about recovery at this point to know that I wasn't able to promise that it wouldn't happen again. I was focused and committed to sobriety, but I also lived in the real world. I knew that a slip-up was possible, and I didn't want to lie to him and pretend that it wasn't. I certainly didn't want to do anything to jeopardize his own sobriety.

I was grateful to remain friends with Alain, but in hindsight it's hard not to feel pain about our relationship ending. We were determined to remain friends - we had both acknowledged and professed that our lives were so much better with the other in it. One weekend, I had to travel back to Vancouver, and we had committed to make time to see each other. It was a beautiful, hot summer day. Alain hadn't been feeling well and was very quiet and introspective, but he was happy to be outside in the glowing warmth of the sun. We spent the day at a lake, taking in the sounds of the children playing nearby, while enjoying a picnic. We swam in the lake, sunbathed out on the dock and later that evening we watched a comedy, one of the many things we loved to do together. We laughed and laughed, forgetting about all our problems and heartaches. We had always had so much fun together. Once the weekend had come to an end, we hugged goodbye. We held each other for what seemed like an eternity, not letting the other break away from the loving grip we shared. I feel so blessed to have had the opportunity to spend that weekend with Alain, not realizing that it would be the last.

We had talked on the phone a few more times in the days after I left, and it was only six short days later that Alain died. It was a sudden coronary issue and it shocked me to my core. Although we weren't together as a couple when he passed, he had quickly become my best friend and confidant. I could rely on him for just about anything. He also showed me how much he cared for me, and he helped me get through one of the hardest years of my life. Our romance was intense, yet so brief. It came and went far too quickly, leaving me with the realization of how fleeting our time on earth can be.

I believe that Alain is an angel, sent to help me through some very dark moments, and then he returned to heaven. He was with me just long enough to make sure that I was okay, and when I was, he took his leave. I truly wish we had more time together, but I know he is at peace and in God's loving embrace. I also take comfort in the many gifts he gave me through knowing him; gifts of knowledge, education on sobriety, and newfound feelings of comfort, trust and confidence in another human being were just a few of the gifts he imparted upon me. He was truly a blessing in my life.

Thirteen: Moving Toward Insight

My hope is that you, my readers, have a deeper understanding of my story about addiction and recovery. It's not just a battle against the death grip of the substance or addiction, nor is it only fighting through the trauma to gain a deeper understanding. It's a much broader experience of key lessons we can take away from our journey. Everyone's story is unique, and no one person's experiences can be generalized as the path forward to recovery for anyone else. With that said, sharing my experience of addiction and recovery is important for creating meaning out of some terrible things that happened in my life. I don't just want to reflect and gain personal insight; my hope is to help others who have gone through and are going through their struggles of recovery.

So, what insights can we glean from my recovery journey? First of all, I believe that being aware of the all-consuming shame that drives your addiction is paramount for anyone going through these kinds of challenges. When we recognize and understand the role that shame plays in addiction, we can inherently empower ourselves. Moreover, by understanding the root cause of our shame, and that shame is driven by our being emotionally or physically abandoned in childhood as well as being subjected to other, lasting traumas throughout our lives, we can forgive ourselves and start to feel human again.

At this point, I want to turn toward the topics of religion and spirituality, but I want to preface my discussion by first saying this: religion and spirituality are very personal topics. I would absolutely hate for a reader to be turned off because their perception of God differs from mine or because they're an atheist and don't even believe in God! You do not need religion, or organized religion, to facilitate your recovery – far from it.

What's most important here is the notion of a *higher power*. For some people, that is God in the traditional Abrahamic sense. For others, it's Buddha. For others still, it's the Universe or the concept of love and that we are all One. Maybe, for you, it's family. Everyone's idea of a higher power is different, and all are valid. So, please understand that when I talk about God, I'm talking about my personal beliefs vis-a-vis a higher power or creator. This may differ from your personal beliefs, and that's okay! What matters is the concept of a higher power and our relationship to It, in spite of how we may conjure it in our minds. So, conceive of God, or your higher power, however you like. The point is that no one should control or direct your relationship with spirituality or tell you it needs to conform to a particular tradition or religious dogma.

With that said, I'd like to talk about my notion of God and how it has helped me to not only maintain my sobriety, but also to achieve insights in terms of my experiences with addiction and recovery. When I think about God, I think about Yahuah, the Father, and Yahusha, the Son. Without going too in-depth on the topics of traditional religions or the origins of Christianity, I describe myself as a follower of His Word.

Organized religion has always played a role in my life. I can't remember a time in childhood when we didn't have some involvement with organized faith, whether it was attending church or observing religious holidays or some other religious practice. My familiarity with organized religion, especially mainstream Catholicism, has bred a fair amount of skepticism and distrust. I have seen, firsthand, the myriad of hypocrisy that gets involved in the man-made structures and institutions that prevail in most mainstream religious traditions.

At the same time, I have a profound sense of spirituality, and I have heard God's voice since I was a small child. I see my faith as a direct link to God. Rather than my faith needing to be mediated by a priest, or some religious architecture, I find my comfort comes from a direct interface with my creator. Aside from providing me with a more spiritually rewarding experience, I feel that this approach allows me to circumnavigate many of the problems associated with organized faith. In this sense, I am the church. I seek to spread the Word and draw people to God through my love, my acts of compassion, and indeed, my sobriety.

My experiences with addiction strengthened and clarified my faith. I have come to learn and understand that reaching out to God in my darkest moments has had a profoundly positive impact on my ability to maintain my sobriety and approach recovery with the right mindset for lasting change. If I could share a message with someone else experiencing similar struggles, it would be my belief that when we truly humble ourselves, we create the space needed for God to come to us and lift our spirit. If you seek him, he will show up for you. I don't pretend to have the answers, but I can categorically tell you that God is real.

On two occasions I have encountered the loving power of God, wherein I physically felt his presence lifting me up from the pits of despair and offering me a chance at salvation. I wrote earlier about the experience on the floor of my kitchen where I heard God speaking to me. But there was one other time. It was two days after my last ceremony in Mexico when I was visited in a dream by Abuela, also called Mother Aya. Abuela means grandmother in Spanish. She is known as Abuela because she represents the feminine energy of life, fulfilling the role of matriarch of the sacred plant family. Much akin to the nurturing love and guidance that a grandmother provides, Abuela gently guides and provides leadership and insight for those ministered to by the medicine. Some people believe that Abuela manifests to them in a form in which they can relate and identify with. Had Abuela been of a masculine form, I may not have been as receptive to his guidance or teachings because of the trauma inflicted upon me in my life by men.

I was staying with my sister after my ceremonies and using the time to integrate some of the lessons that Abuela had imparted upon me. We were sleeping when suddenly, I was jolted from my dream when my mind became aware of a presence. I know that this wasn't a dream because of how it appeared in my mind. For me, dreams appear in a series of distinct black and white images, similar to old-fashioned movie reels. However, this was something different - you could call it a vision or a visitation. Abuela came to me and spoke. With a soft, sweet voice, she instructed me to breathe life into my youngest daughter. I was puzzled, not understanding her directive, when she then demonstrated a long, deep breath followed by an equally long, smooth exhale. Before I realized it, I was imitating her, slowly inhaling and exhaling, my chest softly rising and falling. It must have been with this soft movement and smooth audible breathing that my sister awoke and curiously watched what I was doing. This went on for some time, with each breath flowing easier than the last.

What did she mean? For a while, I wondered if I had misinterpreted her message, but I realized, no, I understood her correctly. But what did it mean? Eventually, I came to understand. Breathing life into my daughter, or indeed, all my children, is about living honestly and authentically and setting the right example for them to be integral. It is about cultivating my spirituality and reaching the potential that God has created for me. Breathing life into them is about honoring them and loving them and supporting them however they need.

In my own journey, my desire for pure, unfiltered truth and knowledge led me to embrace the Cepher Bible, which ultimately predates the King James Bible as the definitive Word of God. It is the original Hebrew text of the Bible, rather than a Greek translation. Studying the original Hebrew text is important to me because I believe the language that we use profoundly shapes our understanding of concepts and meaning.

Personally, I've found reading the original text more rewarding and more spiritually meaningful than translated versions of the original text. This is why I use the names Yahuah and Yahusha. These are the names used in the original work. Getting as close as possible to the source material is important because I don't want my understanding unnecessarily mediated by someone else's understanding.

So, let's talk about how this is relevant to recovery and addiction. There is a substantial body of research pertaining to recovery and the twelve-step approach, most commonly associated with Alcoholics Anonymous and similar groups. Likewise, author John Bradshaw, who I cited earlier in this book, did a great deal to help publicize the efficacy of the traditional twelve-step approach when dealing with addiction and recovery. Indeed, one of the most critical aspects of this approach to promoting recovery is its relationship with religion and spirituality. Traditionally, a twelve-step approach requires the individual to acknowledge a higher power. Again, this doesn't have to be God in the conventional sense or even a religious figure at all. What's important is acknowledging something greater than yourself, something more indelible and eternal than your own transient existence. My own acknowledgment of a higher power has been critical to maintaining my sobriety.

But we need to understand - why is this helpful for recovery? Why does acknowledging a higher power – whatever it is – help us to heal and maintain our sobriety?

Connection – connection to others, to our world, and to God, is of the utmost importance to our humanity. Sometimes, I think of myself as a human being having a spiritual experience and other times, I think of myself as a spiritual being having a human experience. Too often, our traumas – especially those stemming from childhood – cause us to want to take on a kind of inhuman quality. Phrases like "I can't make mistakes" or "I'm a monster for what I've done" play on this idea. In many ways, it becomes easier to see ourselves as more than human or less than human. I'm grateful to John Bradshaw for his work in helping to clarify this and to promote my understanding. The acknowledgment of a higher power – something outside of ourselves and bigger than ourselves – is about restoring and re-positioning our humanity.

Aside from the acknowledgment of a higher power, the traditional twelve-step approach also typically involves working with a sponsor or operating in relation to a community of others experiencing similar hardships. I cannot articulate the degree to which a sponsor-type figure has been critical to my recovery.

During my journey, I did attend formal meetings, which I found tremendously beneficial. At the same time, I didn't attend enough to ever work with a particular sponsor. This wasn't for any reason other than practicality. When I was just a few weeks into this process, I moved, and my new community didn't have local meetings. But I would recommend seeking out this kind of support for anyone struggling. It is undeniably helpful.

I made connections with my own sponsor-type figures. Indeed, I am so grateful that my own journey has brought me into relationships with some brilliant people who have served as truly effective surrogates in this kind of role. Specifically, I'd like to thank my life coach, Jessica Marie, and her Mastermind group of amazing women who were an integral part of my growth and healing. We talk about basically everything as it relates to life and personal development. I've learned that it's not most important to have someone to talk to and share about your recovery specifically; what's most important is making real, satisfying, meaningful connections with others and then maintaining those connections over time. We all need a support system; we are all human. To think that we can make it on our own or that we don't need others is a lie we tell ourselves, one rooted in fear and shame. Our internalized shame drives a fear that we are not worthy of these kinds of connections. If you're struggling with this, just know that you are worthy of connections. The world is a better place with you in it. People want to be connected to you. Undeniably, everyone has something to offer.

Probably the biggest challenge I've faced in recovery relates to healing fractured relationships with my children. All of my children have had to work through a great deal of anger and resentment over some of the choices that I've made. Some of the most important work I've had to do has involved understanding my children's perspectives and recognizing the validity of their feelings. I can't just blame Christopher's lies on why these relationships are strained; that's part of it, but I can't blame this all on him. My descent into addiction had a profound impact on my children, and I live with a tremendous amount of guilt and regret because I wish things had been different.

Moreover, I feel terrible shame for exposing my children to the toxicity, anger, and hurt that was so prevalent in the household during my marriage to Chris. I can remember vicious fights and anger between us that my kids invariably overheard or even witnessed firsthand. I can recall the fighting and conflict that characterized my own household as a child. I feel deep shame that I perpetuated something that can leave real scars on those I love the most in this world.

I don't engage in self-flagellation because I don't think it's particularly productive, either for my relationships with my kids or for my sobriety. But I certainly engage in a great deal of self-reflection and other work aimed at my own growth and my desire to be the best mom and example I can possibly be. My children are incredible. Their strength and love are not only inspiring but a powerful grounding force that keeps me attuned to the goodness and light in the world. I am continually inspired and delighted by who they are becoming as human beings.

I also want to acknowledge that my children have an amazing support system that goes far beyond me. Chris is a good father, and he loves his children. What's more, his new wife is a lovely human being and a good stepmom to my kids, for which I'm grateful.

Fourteen: Pretty Dark Places

The title of this book comes from my understanding of the beauty that we find in our darkest times. It is my sincere hope that nobody experiences what I did in terms of my wrongful arrest, the spiteful treatment from the authorities, or my experiences with infidelity and abusive relationships. Still, many of us do experience these things. Life is fraught with all kinds of challenges, many of which are uniquely painful and difficult to endure. They strain our personal relationships, and they cause emotional turmoil. They highlight and amplify feelings of shame that, for most of us, stem back to childhood.

Unresolved anger also played an important role in my addictions. I was so angry with my being subject to arrest and defamation, subsidized by my own tax dollars, to boot. Every time I'd pick up a newspaper and read something about organized crime groups brazenly engaging in criminality, with no fear of reprisal from police, I'd become incensed. I felt rage – at the police, at the government, at the situation. But instead of dealing with it in a constructive manner, my rage turned inward, fueling deep-seated anger and, ultimately, my addictions.

In the years since, I am happy to say that I have let go of my anger and come to terms with what happened. I am also happy to share that I recently had a very cordial call with Dave over some minor practical matters that had to be dealt with. He apologized, and I was able to tell him about my sobriety. I expressed gratitude for his apology and for showing both remorse and introspection. We ended the call on a positive note, and it gave me a wonderful feeling of closure. I no longer have to carry anger or hostility, or resentment and I was able to genuinely wish him well.

Some of us experience addictions early in life, while others, like myself, experience these problems as adults. In both cases, however, our addictive behaviors are rooted in our unresolved traumas in childhood. The shame we internalize over time fuels our addictions, and our addictions fuel our shame. This is why so many people get trapped in a vicious cycle of addiction and lose their battles before achieving recovery. That was certainly the case for my brother. I believe it was also the case for Alain, who I mourn deeply.

The good news is that when you embrace recovery and start to heal your addictions, you can start the important work on healing other things that negatively affect your interpersonal relationships. In my case, recovery was a precondition for me coming to terms with my codependent tendencies and learning to change both my thought patterns, as well as my behaviors. This is why it's important not to gloss over our childhood traumas. Too often, we are encouraged to ignore our pain or pretend it doesn't matter because it happened a long time ago. This is wrong. Recognizing these patterns and coming to terms with them not only facilitates recovery, it facilitates an opportunity of change and real growth.

I don't want to pretend that reflection – especially reflection after coming out of a serious addiction – is an easy or pleasant process. In many ways, this kind of reflection is far more painful than the pain associated with being addicted and mired in shame. Because, in many ways, the substances we use mute and cover up our feelings. When we stop using, our feelings tend to bubble to the surface. When we engage in reflection, this stirs up our most painful memories and emotions. As a defense mechanism, we naturally want to avoid this kind of pain.

As part of my work embracing these difficult challenges, I've strived to remember something drawn from my relationship with the Lord that provides me with great comfort and strength. God says that he will take all the bad things that happen to us and make something good come out of it. I'm not saying that we deserve the bad things that happen to us or that bad things are inevitable. I'm only talking about seeing beauty realized from the ashes. That was my prayer, especially when I was deeply consumed by my addictions.

While experiencing trauma, shame, addiction – *real darkness* – you can still have a beautiful and successful life. You can be a role model; you can inspire others; you can do whatever it is that speaks to your heart and soul. Addiction is not a life sentence. I am living proof that anyone can do the work to understand the root causes of their shame and the underlying factors that drive addictive behaviors. Simply by understanding shame, we can start to heal ourselves.

Recovery is an ongoing process, it's not a linear transition from one steady state to another. I don't speak with some false authority or confidence or pretend to have all the answers that anyone struggling with addiction might seek. Still, I have come to learn a number of important things about trauma, shame, addiction, and healing. There's no silver bullet. A panacea does not exist. Recovery involves real work, and that work is taxing. Embracing the emotional labor associated with this kind of work is empowering because it imparts you with a remarkable set of skills, not only for maintaining your sobriety but gaining perspective on life in general. I am grateful for my journey. I am grateful for the beauty I have found in the darkness.

In my case, I can easily identify my faith as the overarching factor that has helped me maintain my sobriety. Now, it's not as simple as saying that having faith can keep you sober. Your individual faith depends entirely on how you see yourself and the world. But for me, maintaining my faith and giving trust in a higher power and creator has been profoundly helpful in promoting perseverance and accepting reality as it is, rather than as I'd like it to be.

Afterword

We have explored some pretty dark places. We've also explored some *pretty dark places*. Finding beauty in the darkness and inspiration from our loved ones is about making deliberate choices aimed at promoting happiness and goodness in our lives.

All of us are worthy of recovery. All of us are worthy of joyful, fulfilling lives and meaningful connections to others. You are not excluded from that group. Your life has meaning – there is a reason for your existence, even if you are unable to see it at this time.

If you or someone you love is battling addiction, it is a hard road. But the journey toward recovery is worth it for yourself, for your loved ones, and for all of us.

So many of us are afraid or too proud to ask for help, thinking we can do it on our own. Seeking help is not a weakness – on the contrary – it's a form of strength. It was one very dark and difficult ceremony (it was terrifying actually!) where I saw clearly the depths of my despair and the damage that my lifestyle was having on my life and the lives of those closest to me. In that moment, I realized that I could no longer go on living as I was. I called out for help – to my sister, to the curandera, to God, to anyone who would listen. I first had to get to a pretty dark place, desperate for help, before I was able to realize that Yahuah was already reaching out to me and all I had to do was surrender my brokenness to Him.

While I do not profess to be an expert on the scientific or psychological effects of trauma, I can speak to my experiences and share with you some of the things I learned while educating myself. My hope is that you may recognize the link between your own behavioural tendencies and any trauma you may have experienced in childhood. Education and a willingness to learn is only one way to work through your struggles. Surrender is key.

Over the last decade, there have been substantial advances in the correlation between addiction and childhood trauma. A heartbreaking statement by Dr. Gabor Maté has captured the essence of addiction when he states *"A person who has suffered childhood trauma does not always become an addict. However, an addict has most undoubtedly experienced some form of childhood trauma."* Dr. Maté has worked in the Downtown Eastside (DTES) of Vancouver for several decades, treating trauma and addiction. His most recent book *"the Myth of Normal: Trauma, Illness & Healing in a Toxic Culture"* has shed light on the connection between childhood trauma and the desire to escape the feelings associated with said trauma. Dr. Maté has a wealth of information available to anyone seeking treatment and healing from addiction and trauma and I encourage you to seek out the knowledge and understanding that he provides through his own website and the many podcasts he has presented on (https://drgabormate.com/).

Dr. Maté believes that the source of addiction is not found in genes but in the early childhood environment, and I tend to agree based on my own experiences. When one is subjected to varying forms of trauma, the young brain, unable to fully comprehend the meaning of what's going on, creates behaviours or reactions to help them feel safe and secure. These behaviours, if not dealt with, might lay dormant for quite a while and give off the impression that they are healed, gradually cementing themselves within the physical body. Those dormant behaviours, over time, may develop into symptoms of "dis-ease" leading to physical pain such as arthritis, fibromyalgia, and debilitating stress to name a few. And when these dormant behaviours are triggered, the emotions that we tried to escape from inevitably rise to the surface, causing even more pain. Covering up this pain by numbing ourselves is *indeed* another form of abandonment - self-abandonment - which further exacerbates the trauma cycle. There is a strong connection between emotions and our physical body that many are not aware of, and that science supports. It is this connection that I would encourage anyone to investigate, as it is a vital part of our tri-pillar of well-being: physical, mental, and emotional health.

~ ~ ~

I would not be here today if it wasn't for the support and love and encouragement from my sister, Lisa. Not only has Lisa helped me to gain access to the healing I needed, but she has also helped me with co-writing and editing this project. While this book first started as a vision, I couldn't have done it on my own.

For those of you interested in taking a more unconventional approach to healing and who may feel a calling to connect with sacred medicine, I encourage you to reach out to Lisa. Consciously doing deep inner work is certain to bring about healing and transformation. After several years of working to resolve her own childhood trauma, she has connected with a beautiful community of healers of varying modalities, as well as other modalities that I didn't touch on here, but experienced and can attest to their efficacy in creating lasting change. Lisa can be reached at: chat.canamex@gmail.com. Starting with a retreat and/or multiple ceremonies may be the catalyst needed for greater insight into your life and the change needed to bring about healing.

Another unconventional yet more gentle approach to healing with sacred medicine which has helped to calm my brain chatter and create new neural pathways, is through psilocybin therapy. I recommend education and research into the new, groundbreaking effects of microdosing psilocybin and for any additional information, please reach out to Steve Mather, a main character from the 2020 documentary "*The Psychedelic Frontier*" and a dear family friend who has been a huge support and wealth of knowledge in this arena. Steve can be reached at: https://www.ateze.com.

One of the most difficult lessons I had to learn along my healing journey, was the importance of compassion and forgiveness – for myself. Compassion is my understanding of the incidents that brought me to the depths of my despair, while forgiveness, as Dr. Gabor Maté explains, is *"an act of releasing the weight of resentment and anger that you carry, which often only burdens your own heart. By forgiving, you free yourself from the grip of past hurts and reclaim your peace, rather than allowing pain to define you."* Healing is possible - there is hope for escape from those pretty dark places.